The Lockdown Limericks

Our Covid Story
The First 200 Days

Claire Baldock

ISBN 978-1-716-23017-2

Published January 2021

Preface

Over my entire life, writing a book is something I never imagined I would do. For years I had written bespoke poems for my friends and colleagues on special occasions but never considered producing work for publication. Back in March 2020 when the horror of the Covid 19 pandemic hit us, such a thing couldn't have been further from my mind. I was aware that people were feeling down about what was in store for us and I just wanted to raise a smile every day, if I could, with rhyming observations about our situation. I sent a verse out to friends by email and posted them on my Facebook page every day. After the first one hundred I realized the daily verses had developed a life of their own. They were telling our Covid story here in the UK. They became the "Lockdown Limericks" and span 200 days from 17th March to 2nd October 2020. My thanks go out to all my wonderful and loyal friends who responded to the limericks every day and provided encouragement.

"I dedicate this work to my dearest friend of 45 years, Mary Manning, who lost her battle with cancer on 19th September 2020. Any royalties from this book, after tax, will go to support research into care and treatments for cancer sufferers."

Claire Baldock

17th March 2020 to 31st March 2020

The Covid 19 virus infection has become well established in the UK. No longer possible to ignore, news is dominated by hand washing protocols involving singing Happy Birthday (twice), social distancing and the terrible shortage of toilet rolls. The Prime Minister announces the holding of daily press conferences from Downing Street where we are all acquainted with the virus reproduction number "R". On 24th March full lockdown is introduced but by the end of the month, Boris Johnson, Matt Hancock, Patrick Whitty and Dominic Cummings have all become infected with Covid 19. On the plus side many welcome the Chancellor, Rishi Sunak, announcing big spending plans to protect jobs with his Furlough scheme.

17.03.20

A virus called Covid – nineteen
means hands must be spotlessly clean
Oh how I hate
to self-isolate
I can't go to tea with the Queen

18.03.20

Now Covid-nineteen life controls
Footballers aren't scoring goals
The seventy plus
can't use the bus
and worse, there are no toilet rolls

19.03.20

Each day Boris speaks to the press
He's wearing respectable dress
A smart suit and tie
So please tell me why
is his hair always in such distress

20.03.20

Plants that make automobiles
have a bit of a challenge one feels
becoming the makers
of more ventilators
At least they can give them some wheels

21.03.20

Another thing causing some strains
There are very few aeroplanes
Just one of those things
The environment wins
as nothing's stacked up over Staines

22.03.20

Ladies, we're in for a spell
when we won't be getting Chanel
the ultimate prize
men can give their wives
is a bottle of handwashing gel

23.03.20

If I might have a word
I've been told by a smart little bird
We need a vaccine
before there is seen
immunity shown by the herd

24.03.20

There was a young virus, Corona
Who holidayed with friend, Fiona
No foreign delights
There weren't any flights
So they opted for two weeks in Cromer

25.03.20

To prevent a financial crash
the Chancellor's splashing the cash
Would it be sound
to have a whip round
or would that be a bit rash?

26.03.208

To help you stay virus free
Get plenty of vitamin C
Lemon and Lime
They will do fine
Especially in your G and T

27.03.20

No toilet rolls on display
Need not cause us dismay
To keep our bits clean
if you know what I mean
we should all get a bidet

28.03.20

Johnson, Hancock and Whitty
probably feel a bit shitty
Did they fail to meet
the distance six feet
required of the rest of the city?

29.03.20

Since they've been in the cot
The kids have been hatching a plot
For years they've had plans
to cancel exams
but Covid is over the top

30.03.20

After shelves are filled overnight
The fruit and veg takes a hike
Purchased by louts
but there's always sprouts
So honestly, what's not to like?

31.03.20

Those in power at the top
are all now getting too hot
the virus won't care
how they got there
and whether elected or not

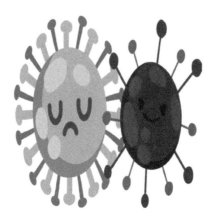

1st April 2020 to 15th April 2020

The difference in the effect of Covid 19, from a mild infection to a very serious and sometimes fatal illness, is starkly demonstrated when Prince Charles catches the virus and makes a quick recovery while Boris the PM has to be admitted to intensive care and administered oxygen. Not only that, but we experience the irony of the best Easter weather we can ever remember but can't go anywhere because everything is closed! Scotland hits the headlines when Nicola Sturgeon sacks her Chief Scientific Officer for travelling to her holiday home against lockdown rules. On the plus side lockdown is ended in Wuhan, China.

01.04.20

Now with the closure of schools
and adopting of new fiscal rules
It's such a high price
Wouldn't it be nice
if Corona was just April fools

02.04.20

The bin collection advice
the Council change in a trice
So what colour bin
to put out or leave in
is just a roll of the dice

03.04.20

Now that the pub's out of bounds
and other social surrounds
we'll find such a move
will savings improve
as we won't have to buy any rounds

04.04.20

There was a young virus, Corona
Turned out a bit of a roamer
She would stop her run
if deal could be done
She's waiting for Boris to phone her

05.04.20

Now they've closed all the links
the golfer's social life shrinks
But now we've the chance
to really advance
our skill set at tiddlywinks

06.04.20

Poor Boris, life's become hard
Now Covid is marking your card
Boris, be brave
We need you to save
the people from Dominic Raab

07.04.20

Corona is just so perverse
Poor Boris is just getting worse
It would be for the best
if he would just rest
and hand over power to the nurse

08.04.20

With Corona virus attack
Doctors, the hospitals lack
To fix the shortfall
they put out a call
and got some old wrinkly ones back

09.04.20

There once was a virus Corona
Got some new genes from a donor
No longer SARS
She cleared out the bars
and adopted a whole new persona

10.04.20

The Scottish lady had flown
away to her holiday home
She had police on her back
Then she'd get the sack
You could tell by Nicola's tone

11.04.20

Covid has made me much wiser
on the use of hand sanitizer
it gives such dry skin
so you must rub in
plenty of nice moisturizer

12.04.20

It's Easter so might I suggest
we get dressed in our Sunday best
I know we're all home
and just with our own
but don't slob around in your vest

13.04.20

Even Prince Charles stayed at home
It seems he became virus prone
Though Covid defining
her high social climbing
she will not ascend to the throne

14.04.20

Corona drank Margarita
along with a chicken fajita
the Mexican food
deadened her mood
I think that's how we'll defeat her!

15.04.20

China's lockdown is suspended
In Wuhan freedom's extended
Now they have oodles
of takeaway noodles
I'm sure they'll be very soon mended

16th April 2020 to 30th April 2020

We learn that our lockdown is to be extended by a further three weeks. Given that the number of infections continues to rise steeply, this is hardly a surprise. PPE shortages are continuing and President Trump suggests we inject bleach to combat the infection. Notwithstanding all this, many more encouraging things happen in the second half of April including the opening of the first of the new Nightingale hospitals in the converted ExCeL Conference Centre, extra ventilators designed by the Mercedes and McLaren Formula One teams are ready for delivery, the fabulous veteran Captain Tom Moore raises money for the NHS by walking around his garden, a huge reduction in air pollution is reported and Boris recovers from his Covid ordeal. More good news late in April when Boris's fiancé Carrie safely gives birth to their son Wilfred.

16.04.20

A hospital built in nine days
has thousands of medical bays
Once no longer sick
you won't get out quick
I've heard it's a bit of a maze

17.04.20

Lockdown to last three more weeks
Deprived of all social treats
But there's always Zoom^R
if not in same room
and Messenger, WhatsApp^R and tweets

18.04.20

There's more ventilation for some
Made by Formula One
They produced super quick
Didn't stop in the pit
In just a few laps it was done

19.04.20

My Mum has come up with a gem
There won't be a crime wave to stem
No burglars about
as we're not going out
Will Chancellor have package for them?

20.04.20

One of the things that's a blow
I can't to the hairdresser go
Soon I'll declare
I have Boris's hair
and all my grey's going to show

21.04.20

Let's hear it for good Captain Tom
So steadily walking along
He must be praised
for the money he's raised
with such courage, style and aplomb

22.04.20

The World Health Organization
has fallen out with a nation
Though it's income falls
Not taking Trump's calls
Too busy with vaccine creation

23.04.20

We're searching in every time zone
For PPE far from home
But there's companies here
who can make all this gear
Matt Hancock, please pick up the phone!

24.04.20

Covid it seems lays to waste
your senses, so you can't taste
It will be hell
when you can't tell
chocolate sauce from toothpaste

25.04.20

In test kits we have invested
so thousands more might be tested
and then contacts traced
a strategy based
on something Korea suggested

26.04.20

I hope there's a point we can reach
where there's medication for each
We can cure Covid ills
by taking some pills
but please don't ever drink bleach!

27.04.20

PM is back in the saddle
He can in governance dabble
The others all speak
but we seem up the creek
Is PM the one with the paddle?

28.04.20

The PM it seems has now found
you can wrestle Covid to the ground
A better suggestion
than bleach for ingestion
Least more metaphorically sound

29.04.20

There's been a great diminution
in quantities of air pollution
more birdlife is here
more bluebells and deer
Such a wildlife revolution

30.04.20

Boris, a father again
Without any bongs from Big Ben
A new born for Carrie
and rival to Larry
for cuddles within Number Ten

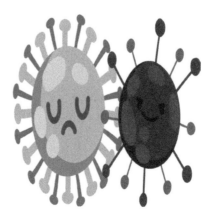

1st May 2020 to 15th May 2020

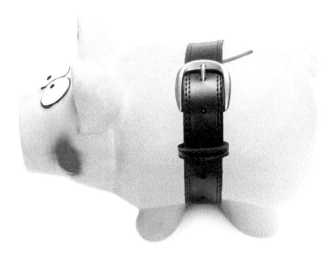

Many people are starting to confuse their seasonal hay fever symptoms with Covid 19 infection. There is a drive for more testing and the military are assisting with mobile testing units. Our world-beating track and trace App is starting its trial on the Isle of Wight. The 8th May is the VE Day celebration leading to wild street parties and some rather dodgy social distancing. We are told that we must be alert! Though masks are not mandatory, many are sewing them at home and making them a fashion statement. Despite all this positivity forecasts for the economy start to become very gloomy.

01.05.20

Our air is not totally clear
Still particle-filled atmosphere
Not Covid nineteen
Too much histamine
The hay fever season is here

02.05.20

To testing requirements fulfil
we're using Military skill
There'll be a man
pops round in a van
to test all those that are ill

03.05.20

Spare time, so let's decorate?
Paint while we self-isolate
But I've no compulsion
to spread the emulsion
even though hall's in a state

04.05.20

Now the Government vows
to have an app that allows
tracing infection
with Bluetooth^R connection
but only if you're in Cowes

05.05.20

A drug called Remdesivir
might breach the Covid frontier
If experts agree
on the efficacy
it would give us something to cheer

06.05.20

There is some new facial gear
with straps which go over each ear
You must not go out
without this on your snout
as that would be just so last year

07.05.20

During this difficult patch
We can't the new fashion trends catch
So nothing too rogue
but according to Vogue[R]
your outfit and face mask must match

08.05.20

Free of the battles that drove her
The war in Europe was over
Old Blighty could sing
with dear Vera Lynn
of birds over White Cliffs of Dover

09.05.20

Hollywood should make a start
and practice their film making art
the whole Covid story
would bring Oscar glory
for the one that gets Covid's part

10.05.20

A film about Covid nineteen
will just on Netflix^R be seen
The problem exposed
is cinema's closed
It can't be on the big screen

11.05.20

Though certainly not a dead cert
The young might go back to work
The oldies won't dare
nod off in the chair
as now we must all be alert!

12.05.20

As end of lockdown we seek
live golf on the telly next week
Just four pros seek glory
We'll shout "come on Rory"
I'm setting Sky Q^R as we speak

13.05.20

Rishi's Furlough extension
aims at employment retention
He found extra quota
down back of the sofa
to fund this new intervention

14.05.20

Financial anxieties rise
We hear the economists' cries
that Covid ingression
will cause huge recession
Oh really? Now there's a surprise!

15.05.20

Now you can buy property
although you will not be free
to go round the place
or evaluate space
Just virtual visits you see

16th May 2020 to 30th May 2020

Garden Centres and Golf courses open up! I play my first round for 8 weeks but find lockdown has done nothing to improve my woeful standard. There is a lot of wild life on the golf course and in our garden due to decreased pollution levels. As a result, our usually lazy cat, brings in a bird and leaves it on the living room carpet. There is however lack of life, wild or otherwise, in the Houses of Parliament as social distancing means most MPs are at home attending virtually. Track and trace system (without the App), begins. Captain Tom is awarded a Knighthood. News however is dominated in late May buy the actions of the PM's political advisor Dominic Cummings, who travelled to his parents' home in County Durham while infected with Covid 19, allegedly in breach of lockdown regulations.

16.05.20

Now nurseries you can go in
and keep the garden in trim
but with all that mowing
and weeding and hoeing
I hope they collect your green bin

17.05.20

I think I know of a place
where Covid there's not yet a trace
We could vacation
upon the space station
Tim Peake says it's just ace

18.05.20

As holiday time starts to loom
Get arranging quite soon
For avoiding infection
another suggestion
two weeks in a hot air balloon

19.05.20

To get your test results fast
dogs might be up to the task
For Covid detection
they'd sniff the infection
Now wouldn't that be a blast

20.05.20

Parliament's lacking some drama
The atmosphere couldn't be calmer
A cavernous room
with MPs on Zoom^R
except the PM and Kier Starmer

21.05.20

Captain Tom Moore has been knighted
He says he's really delighted
Although he can't kneel
he will seal the deal
when by the Queen he's invited

22.05.20

I went out to play golf yesterday
A disappointing display
Lockdown has not
improved any shot
No scorecards though, so that's OK

23.05.20

Could we print more cash for the nation?
I know it increases inflation
But we're going to get
billions in debt
to be paid by the next generation

24.05.20

Dom the government aide
has done what I thought he forbade
In infectious mode
he got on the road
and Cummings and goings were made!

25.05.20

Public transport of course
No longer a useful resource
Walk if you like
or get on your bike
on roller blades or on a horse

26.05.20

The PM's been busy of late
considering Dominic's fate
Then there's Carrie and Dilyn
and Covid the villain
and Wilfred to keep him awake

27.05.20

More shops will be open in June
We'll have a chance to consume
You can buy a bra
or maybe a car
but a haircut? Not any time soon!

28.05.20

Though some of our freedoms are rising
Still don't have enough exercising
So many foods now
I cannot allow
to avoid disastrous upsizing

29.05.20

Tracking and tracing begins
If with someone for fifteen mins
and they're not Covid free
you will soon be
stuck at home drinking the gins!

30.05.20

Our cat has brought in a bird
So I have been having a word
I began my address
"Look at that mess!"
She just took no notice and purred

31st May 2020 to 14th June 2020

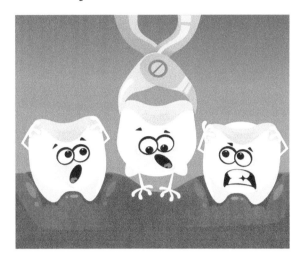

It seems we could be over the peak. There is still a tragic daily death toll but the infection rate is dropping and our friend R falls below 1 (well everywhere except the Northwest that is). The Government succumbs to the temptation to open up the economy and they start with the Dentists – oh joy! Shops selling non-essential items are to follow so we can all go out and buy the non-essential things we don't actually need. The bubble concept is emerging and sadly, is not about drinking more Prosecco. MPs are back to demonstrate their Britishness by queuing in endless socially distanced lines to get into the division lobbies and vote. Introduction of 14 days quarantine if arriving from abroad by the Home Secretary is most unpopular with the travel industry.

31.05.20

Seems we can all barbeque
At home have a bit of a do
But just with five mates
bring your own plates
and don't go using the loo

01.06.20

They're opening some of the schools
with social distancing rules
so next generation
will get education
and won't grow up to be fools

02.06.20

Mum has been round for a cuppa
Something her shielding did scupper
To avoid Covid bug
she brought her own mug
and went home again for her supper

03.06.20

Seems some in the SAGE meeting room
think lockdown has ended too soon
So we are desirous
regarding the virus
to know what stance to assume

04.06.20

Some MPs will now vote
on legislation of note
by queueing for miles
in small little aisles
without the tech that's bespoke

05.06.20

Alok does not have CV
but got me thinking you see
If minister falls
will track and trace calls
go to every MP?

06.06.20

Corona's not much of a laugh
But it's going down on the graph
So not pessimistic
about each statistic
well at least not the government staff

07.06.20

Coronas on surfaces lurk
They'll be there when you're back to work
So most vital task
Put on a mask
but first give the handwash a squirt

08.06.20

Today the dentist is back
I hope you haven't been slack
They will be cross
if you've not had a floss
and removed all your tartar and plaque

09.06.20

Should you go away for a spell
You'll be facing quarantine hell
Airlines are cross
at financial loss
especially with Priti Patel

10.06.20

Recently in the North West
R was not looking it's best
It had the potential
to go exponential
and spread our unwanted guest

11.06.20

The plan for school kids to learn
to study in this Summer term
made teachers tut
It all went tits-up
and Boris has done a U-turn

12.06.20

I don't think I'll ever again
check myself in for a plane
Could be single rider
upon a hang glider
though suitcases would be a pain

13.06.20

We're now permitted to huddle
but it is a bit of a muddle
getting etiquette right
on who to invite
to join you inside your bubble

14.06.20

Tomorrow we'll have more retail
Some non-essentials for sale
When in each store
there'll be marks on the floor
You'll have to follow the trail

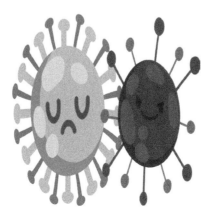

15th June 2020 to 29th June 2020

We pass 100 days of our Covid experience and Boris decides to drop the daily press conferences in case we are getting bored. The drive to open things up continues. We can go to Zoos, Safari Parks and places of worship. Bars and restaurants come back on stream as long as you have ID. The medics have found that a cheap known steroid drug called dexamethasone is reducing the ventilation needed to the sickest patients. Brilliant! Premiership football is back in empty stadiums and what's more gives back when Marcus Rashford persuades the PM to feed hungry school children during lockdown. Sad news is that the NHS Track and Trace App turns out to be useless (at least in Cowes) and just weeks after the VE day celebration, dear Dame Vera passes away at the amazing age of 103.

15.06.20

Now we can go to the Zoo
Safari parks we can drive through
Giraffes cannot shirk
and Lions back to work
It seems their Furlough ends too

16.06.20

Soon we'll be getting our kicks
with a pleasant night out at the flicks
films will be thrivin'
when watched at the drive-in
with bag of their best pick 'n mix

17.06.20

Professional football is planned
without any crowd in the stand
No hugs in relation
to goal celebration
as being a wuss will be banned

18.06.20

Best Covid development yet
Old steroid seems a good bet
Cuts lung inflammation
when on ventilation
but won't increase NHS debt

19.06.20

Rashford the footballing star
has raised the political bar
His enormous compassion
got school kids food ration
A Knighthood for him can't be far

20.06.20

Tributes this week to Dame Vera
Sweetheart of World War two era
She brought many joys
to her own Forces' boys
Her message could not have been clearer

21.06.20

Hancock is now in disgrace
There isn't an app that can trace
no evolution
of hi-tech solution
Just person you meet face to face

22.06.20

If mask is worn on the plane
it seems we can all go to Spain
Have Sangria spree
It's quarantine free
except when we come home again!

23.06.20

The two-meter gap to be seated
has pubs and restaurants defeated
but should we approve
the one-meter move
if Covid has not yet retreated?

24.06.20

One hundred verses today
and press briefings going away
Ministers seem
to have run out of steam
So I'll keep the news on display

25.06.20

The clergy we will now permit
to sermonize from the pulpit
but worshipers few
must each have own pew
to sit or lie down for a bit

26.06.20

To maintain their position of trust
Guide dogs will have to adjust
For keeping their master
from Covid disaster
the social distance a must

27.06.20

The government says we can meet
in restaurants and bars from next week
A question I ask
If wearing mask
how are we all going to eat?

28.06.20

When you go into a bar
You'll need ID for a jar
Probably right
as by end of night
you might not know who you are!

29.06.20

As lockdown begins to relent
You can have a cottage to rent
hotel by the sea
or AirBnB^R
or if you prefer just a tent

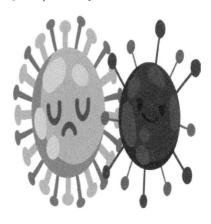

30ᵗʰ June 2020 to 14ᵗʰ July 2020

We start to be confused about the conflicts facing us as the race to open up goes at full speed. Gyms and pools open, we can get married, have a haircut and "Eat Out to Help Out" with nothing to stop us enjoying all of those things in the same day if we want to. It is suggested that after 6ᵗʰ July "shielded" people might like to go to the shops (to buy non-essential things perhaps?). At the same time rates of infection are increasing with all this activity and we have to experiment with local lockdown. There is no tennis at Wimbledon either. I repeat - THERE IS NO WIMBLEDON. Arrrh!! Concern about the economy is continuing to worry those that know about these things and so Rishi announces he will borrow lots more money to cheer everyone up.

30.06.20

Inside meetings are planned
but more than two families banned
So you can insist
to strike off the list
all of those folks you can't stand!

01.07.20

Covid continues to fester
Oh my, how much we detest her
Now a hotbed
where virus has spread
means local lockdown in Leicester

02.07.20

On lawns of South West nineteen
No Novak, no Rafa, no Theim
No umpires, no balls
No challenged line calls
No Pimm's^R or strawberries and cream

03.07.20

For shielding the end is soon nigh
as from the 6th of July
the shielded might mix
outside with six
if Covid is not passing by

04.07.20

The easing of lockdown provisions
means lots of awkward decisions
Would staying in
with bottle of gin
be safer than these new permissions?

05.07.20

As out of lockdown we head
It seems you're allowed to get wed
Exchange wedding bands
with sanitized hands
and guests who are socially spread

06.07.20

The Chancellor wants to avoid
too many folks unemployed
So Job Centre figure
for budget much bigger
than formerly they had enjoyed

07.07.20

To start a full school regimen
there's bubble theory again
If you put in the lot
won't it go pop?
It's just a question of when

08.07.20

I'm having a haircut today
Hip hip, hip hip, hooray!
I'm going to disguise
with selection of dyes
the fact that I'm really so grey!

09.07.20

So restaurant trade will be brisk
and Covid fear be dismissed
We're getting a tenner
Oh what a dilemma
in judging the eating out risk

10.07.20

Chancellor is giving attention
to aiding employment retention
by making a splash
and borrowing cash
in amounts too scary to mention

11.07.20

In Scotland now in the shops
Don't get caught by the cops
North of the border
Executive order
means must have mask on your chops

12.07.20

Soon we can go to the gym
Be all toned and get slim
Tackle the issue
of adipose tissue
from lockdown dietary sin!

13.07.20

The day is about to arrive
when pools to open will strive
they will have to alter
where they put the water
It's just in lanes one, three and five!

14.07.20

The drug called Remdesivir
can breach the Covid frontier
But access denying
US panic buying
means there'll be no benefit here

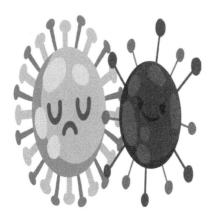

15th July 2020 to 29th July 2020

Boris is victorious over Michael Gove in a row about the wearing of face masks in the shops in England. Once the policy is adopted, a range of personal styles are displayed and going to the supermarket is much more interesting. We see more openings - National Trust properties, outdoor theatres and tattoo parlours - yet we still stay at home and drink more tea. Medical topics are dominating the news. A team at Oxford University releases promising results for its anti-Covid 19 vaccine and the anti-viral protein interferon makes a comeback as a possible treatment. Not so good is that the Russians are apparently hacking into our vaccine research and we have overstated the death figures due to a quirk in the reporting. Captain Tom though continues to ride high and receives his Knighthood from the Queen at Windsor Castle on a sunny day – Lovely.

15.07.20

At last a mask wearing drill
to stop us all getting ill
such vacillation
confusing the nation
Now Boris one, Michael Gove nil!

16.07.20

For homes of the National Trust
opening cannot be rushed
So just a few
will be able to view
each painting, statue or bust

17.07.20

Just between me and you
I'm not going to get a tattoo
Though many enjoy
I'm a bit coy
so I'll stick to flesh-coloured hue

18.07.20

Memories were made yesterday
at a castle that's down Windsor way
Her Majesty's greeting
a personal meeting
when Captain Tom Moore got his K

19.07.20

The Russians it seems have been hacking
and all of our vaccine work tracking
Vladimir Putin
is putting the boot in
Is cybersecurity lacking?

20.07.20

Pretty soon we'll be getting
theatricals in outside setting
as there's no roof
take waterproof
or trip you might be regretting

21.07.20

A vaccine from Oxford, UK
looked rather good yesterday
Hope we know soon
if we can be immune
and contemplate safe holiday

22.07.20

Corona likes riding her bike
out cycling with her friend Spike
So all it requires
is to let down their tyres
and then they could both take a hike!

23.07.20

In lockdown the drinking of tea
increased by a massive degree
More biscuits were sunk
We're so keen to dunk
That's typically British you see

24.07.20

Covid has found a new treat
in plants that are processing meat
if the solution
is veg substitution
will butchers be feeling the heat?

25.07.20

The transition to masks has been made
In every colour and shade
The tight and the baggy
The crisp and the saggy
Oh what a fashion parade!

26.07.20

The Government wants to accrue
plenty of vaccine for flu
Covid's enough
to make you feel rough
without influenza here too

27.07.20

Spain has more Covid nineteen
and Gov re-imposed quarantine
so time won't be lacking
for travellers unpacking
and loading the washing machine

28.07.20

Virologists, oh how they've jumped
so that the virus is dumped
Now interferon
is getting its gear on
ensuring that Covid gets thumped

29.07.20

Seems English Covid death figure
has not been prepared with much rigour
It has those passed on
when Covid long gone
making our death toll seem bigger

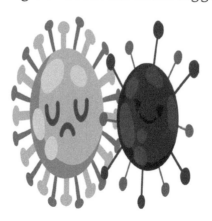

30th July 2020 to 13th August 2020

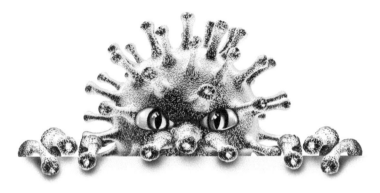

Infections rates are rising and our friend R is back in the news after a long absence. The Government's opening up plans are taking a few blows. Households can no longer mix in Northern England, restaurants close in Aberdeen and those returning from France must now quarantine for 14 days. There is a suggestion the over 50s should stay in! Professor Whitty says that if schools are to open for the Autumn, recreational venues might have to close, presumably so that all the Covid spreading is done by school kids. Things are even worse for the Government as there is an absolutely huge debacle about the A level results because there haven't actually been any A levels and they have to be made up. Absolutely everyone has an opinion as to how this should be done!

30.07.20

Corona is such a marauder
and causes a lot of disorder
Could we stop her capers
by seizing her papers
so she can't sneak in through the border?

31.07.20

The South Ken museums now call
to each vast exhibiting hall
Dinosaurs dressed
in their Sunday best
All ready to greet one and all

01.08.20

We won't be playing roulette
or doing an ice pirouette
nor ten pin bowling
won't see those balls rolling
nor watching for pins to reset

02.08.20

Northern increased virus rates
means you can't visit your mates
Jolly good too
as they won't have to do
the housework your visit creates

03.08.20

Boris predicts second wave
The nation will have to behave
Protocol stands
Wear masks and wash hands
and distance if out at a rave

04.08.20

It seems to preserve education
and Covid disorientation
whether Vicar or tart
you must stay apart
and try to avoid recreation

05.08.20

I read in the news yesterday
the over fifties should stay
shielded at home
Oh how we'll moan
Can't recall rules anyway!

06.08.20

Oh how virologists rock!
There's a new test on the block
A portable kit
detects double quick
That'll give Covid a shock!

07.08.20

Pupils are getting assessed
without the exams to get stressed
For this generation
a good commendation
depends if the teacher's impressed!

08.08.20

I was surprised I must say
at comeback for R yesterday
Favoured by geeks
yet absent for weeks
Hope it had nice holiday

09.08.20

Resurgence of Covid nineteen
closed restaurants in Aberdeen
Now far too risky
to go out for whisky
a deep-fried Mars or ice cream

10.08.20

A recent mask acquisition
was found in defective condition
One fifty mil
and they don't fit the bill
for either the nurse or clinician

11.08.20

More lockdown in Wales is now gone
for swimming pools closed for so long
But please don't assume
there'll be changing room
Arrive there with your cozzie on!

12.08.20

Now it seems you must wear
a face cover when you're at prayer
You can't reveal
ecumenical zeal
whichever religion you share

13.08.20

So now there is such a furore
about pupils' A level score
If they get shocks
they'll rely on their mocks
to put up their grades a bit more

14th August 2020 to 28th August 2020

The row about the Exams rumbles on and turns to the question of "the algorithm", a word I had hoped I would never have to rhyme. The Head of the Exams regulator resigns. Also, a new educational row has broken out about whether face masks are needed in school when the new term begins. There is a Covid spike in a sandwich factory in Northampton and a need for more lockdown measures in Birmingham. We are trillions in debt. Boris goes on holiday. On the science side of things, R is up but deaths are down, we are going to be randomly tested in our homes, the Russians reckon they have a working vaccine and it is reported that Covid does things to your sense of taste and smell that other, more wimpy viruses cannot reach.

14.08.20

For those that are now "en vacances"
enjoying the French ambiance
substantial re-birth
of Covid dix-neuf
means La quarantine's our response

15.08.20

The Russians now have a vaccine
They say it stops Covid nineteen
but tests did comprise
a small sample size
and not a conventional scheme

16.08.20

Williamson faces derision
for every exam grade decision
as too much downgrading
means Uni hopes fading
due to Ofqual algorithm

17.08.20

No matter how much they might whine
Non-mask-wearing is out of line
You'll be in a bind
if you've left mask behind
You'll have to face gigantic fine

18.08.20

With A level U-turn last night
the Gov tries to put problems right
as flawed regulation
to stop grade inflation
so many prospects would blight

19.08.20

Spas open to help you relax
with whichever massage attracts
to stimulate muscles
and excite corpuscles
while beautician fills facial cracks!

20.08.20

So Covid testing now grows
and just to add to our woes
Someone knocks at your door
you cannot ignore
and sticks a swab up your nose!

21.08.20

Northampton has twelfth highest rate
in Covid infection of late
in plant that makes packs
of M&S[R] snacks
it thought it would go replicate

22.08.20

With Covid you have to endure
that number of taste buds are fewer
and unlike the flu
you won't have a clue
you're next to a bag of manure

23.08.20

So now we're two trillion in debt
and we've not conquered Covid just yet
Rishi's tried hard
but maxed out on the card
and needs credit limit re-set

24.08.20

Boris has been on vacation
while crisis within education
Hope 5G installed
for when Gavin called
for awkward and long conversation!

25.08.20

It seems there is now no disguising
that value of R has been rising
yet hospitalized
has really downsized
That's good and rather surprising

26.08.20

So Whitty, the medical preacher
says Covid's not such a creature
to do school kids harm
no need for alarm
but who's looking after the teacher!

27.08.20

So should they wear face masks in school?
Just what is a suitable rule?
Kids follow trends
and care for their friends
but would prefer mask that looks cool!

28.08.20

More Covid infection in Brum
There might be more lockdown to come
So Dudley and Aston
and maybe Edgbaston
will not be having much fun

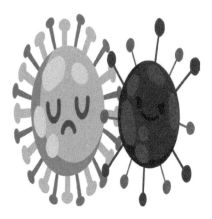

29th August 2020 to 12th Sept 2020

Infection continues to rise again around the world and the number of countries on our quarantine list keeps increasing, although it does depend where in the UK you actually want to arrive. Notwithstanding, Grant Shapps, the Transport Minister, allows the introduction of regional air "corridors" making travel even more complicated. We are reminded that, as Winter approaches, Covid will not be the only bug on the block to make you ill. Well ventilated work environments are encouraged but it probably doesn't matter as many are wedded to the "working at home" arrangements and won't be returning to the office any time soon. As September progresses rising infection rates cause Boris to announce the "Rule of Six" where only six people may mix indoors or outdoors. The many exceptions to this rule are quite bewildering.

29.08.20

An organization maligned
the head of Ofqual resigned
No politician
would make this decision
as morals more loosely defined

30.08.20

The practice of working from home
Covid's ensured that it's grown
No need for smart dress
Just have to impress
your Laptop and your mobile phone

31.08.20

In Winter we must provide
good ventilation inside
Covid gets huffy
when indoors not stuffy
and might not care to reside

01.09.20

The Autumn term is now here
Some last-minute rules did appear
If Covid troubles
schools chuck out whole bubbles
How they will learn is not clear

02.09.20

If you've been away getting tanned
in a tropical far away land
Now new Covid risk
on the quarantine list
is the place where Bob Marley once jammed!

03.09.20

Families must remain solo
and mixing households a no no
as Covid is rising
there's no compromising
in Bolton, Trafford and Glasgow

04.09.20

At Christmas we'll have a jug
of mulled wine that we can glug
but not that much passion
as just one hug ration
and only if free of the bug!

05.09.20

So quarantine now after flights
might be beach of our human rights
The case to be fought
in the English High Court
means legal bills reaching new heights

06.09.20

Doctors are really so clever
Now they've got treatments together
which seem to suppress
the number of deaths
and thwart Covid's evil endeavor

07.09.20

There was young virus Corona
who found a new host to re-home her
where she hoped to write
but just out of spite
the printer had run out of toner

08.09.20

We learned we can use yesterday
corridors when we're away
Not over the moon
I'd prefer proper room
in hotel when I'm going to stay

09.09.20

Covid's been up to her tricks
and extra freedom restricts
Unless it is sport
you can only cavort
indoors or outdoors with six

10.09.20

Corona is hoping to learn
For education she'll yearn
So infection pressure
if Covid's a fresher
in new University term

11.09.20

We now to the winter transition
and Covid will face competition
from bugs that are old
the flu, common cold
which could knock her off top position

12.09.20

Covid is going on "Strictly"
She'll plaster the make-up on thickly
If Craig won't approve
her American smooth
she'll probably make him quite sickly

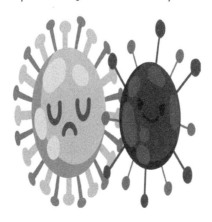

13th Sept 2020 to 2nd Oct 2020

We are moving to the expected second Covid wave and R is back in the news again every day. Infections are rising exponentially in many parts of the UK and residents are now thrown out of the pubs at 10.00pm. There is toilet roll stockpiling again. Cracks are appearing in the testing system. Marshals may patrol the streets soon to break up crowds and big fines are imposed for not isolating if told to do so. Students at University are locked in and Boris is proposing a "circuit breaker" although we don't quite know what that means. It seems we are back where these limericks began. We have come full circle. WE HAVE THE APP THOUGH! I have downloaded it and think I have just about worked out how to use it. Will that be the answer?

13.09.20

We might get a test every day
so we can go out to play
without the insistence
of full social distance
but billions of quid in outlay!

14.09.20

The App's back on the agenda
This time put out to tender
so there's compliance
with major tech giants
Be ready the end of September

15.09.20

Watch for hands, face and space
A rhyme that we must embrace
We can't get too far
in lowering R
without a good slogan in place!

16.09.20

The testing system for Covid
is starting to be overloaded
Appointments online
booked up all the time
and confidence is now eroded

17.09.20

*Now we have "Rule of Six" blues
as extra restriction accrues
diverged regulations
in all the home nations
has plenty of scope to confuse*

18.09.20

*Theatre opening approved
Stage shows can now be viewed
Interval wine
must be ordered online
and some of the seats are removed*

19.09.20

*For viral transmission to block
In North East at ten o'clock
a curfew's imposed
and pubs are all closed
to stop Covid running amok*

20.09.20

*There are plenty of swabs for a test
It's just they can't get assessed
It would be fab
if more in the lab
to see that the problem's addressed*

21.09.20

As Covid continues to spread
the thing that fills us with dread
and scares number ten
is lockdown again
as we're too much in the red

22.09.20

In view of new Covid data
PM suggests circuit breaker
so all predictions
are that new restrictions
will be with us sooner or later

23.09.20

We're getting a Marshal or two
in a city centre near you
They'll keep on the lid
if crowds get too big
by standing around going "shoo"!

24.09.20

New self-isolation rule planned
so Covid won't get out of hand
There's a new fine
needs large bottom line
as breach will cost you ten grand!

25.09.20

So extra decisions in store
as Covid transmission's now more
when should you try
to turn a blind eye
and when should you grass-up next door?!

26.09.20

The Covid fires we must douse
by staying around in the house
we're just allowed six
in each social mix
except when you're going to shoot grouse!

27.09. 20

They've cancelled the budget this year
Taxes won't rise we all cheer
But too many knocks
for Rishi's Red Box
He's spent all the money, oh dear!

28.09.20

Now we have track and trace App
which we are encouraged to tap
oh what a pest
if positive test
it seems that you can't enter that!

29.09.20

I said in a verse back in May
sniffer dogs could lead the way
they've done rather well
they can Covid smell
but woof is all they can say!

30.09.20

Students have not much to cheer
Especially those in their first year
Poor undergrads
Will their Mums and Dads
heed their request to bring beer?!

01.10.20

With Covid testing delay
Experts look for new way
The bug's a survivor
within the saliva
so now we must spit for UK!

02.10.20

Two hundred verses now written
and Covid still bothering Britain
You've all been fantastic
and enthusiastic
so volume two now my ambition!

Claire Baldock is a retired Patent Attorney and lives in Hazlemere, Bucks with her husband Graham and their black and white cat Magic.

DUGONGS

Dugongs, dugongs, how they swim,
In a race, they'll always win.

I love the way their bodies move,
In a disco, they'll have the best groove.

Dugong's smile is so lovely and bright,
They shine more than Jesus, they give off the light.

Dugongs, dugongs, they should not die,
It's not fair for them, to say goodbye.

So please, please, please, keep the water clean,
Because if they die, it's because of human beings.

How dugongs Hoover up grass, is a cool way to eat,
Good job they don't really eat meat.

Dugongs . . .
Dugongs . . .
Dugongs!

Isaac Saint

IN THE SUMMER

In the summer I go to France
In the summer I like to dance

In the summer I love to sing
In the summer I like to swing

In the summer I eat ice cream
In the summer I love to scream

In the summer I love to talk
In the summer I like to walk

In the summer I feel so happy
Because I always see my granny.

Chloe Anne Heaton (9)

CINDERELLA

There was a girl called Cinderella,
Who bagged herself a charming fella.
So this is how the story started,
Her two ugly sisters were very cold hearted.
An invitation came through the door,
Inviting to the ball no more than four.
But the sisters did not want Cinders to attend,
So they tore up the invite; it was unable to mend.
Cinderella, so upset, started to cry,
As her ugly step sisters waved goodbye.
But later that night, after they had left for the ball,
A strange old woman lurked in the hall.
Cinders shouted, 'Who are you? Who are you?'
'I'm your Fairy Godmother,' she replied, 'here to make your dreams come true.'
Then the lady revealed her magic wand,
Cinderella was in shock, unable to respond.
With one quick flash, the makeover was complete,
Cinderella glowed from head to feet.
Then with a zap and a whoosh a carriage appeared,
As Cinders dried her happy tears.
Cinderella's eyes had started to glisten,
But the Fairy Godmother whispered, 'Listen, dear, listen.
All that is good, will not be for long,
Leave the ball at midnight, or everything will go wrong.'
As Cinderella arrived at the ball,
She felt like she was a fly on the wall.
But when the Prince approached and asked her to dance,
Happiness filled the air, as did romance.
But when midnight emerged and the clock struck,
Cinderella realised she had run out of luck.
And as the words of the fairy filled her mind,
She fled to the exit leaving her glass slipper behind.
As the morning came, Cinderella sobbed,
Feeling like her true love had been robbed.
But when the Prince arrived holding her shoe
Her evil sisters locked her in a room out of view.
One tried on the slipper but it was far too small,
And for the other it was too big, making her fall.
But then Cinders broke free from the room she'd been kept,
And at sight of the Prince, she almost wept.
So Cinderella slipped on the dainty glass shoe,
And at last Cinder's dreams of love came true.
The prince took her hand and presented the ring,

She was soon to be queen, and he to be king.
So Prince Charming and Cinderella got wed,
And the magical words 'I love you' were said.
There was smiling and happiness and lots of laughter,
As the Prince and Cinderella lived happily ever after.

Rhea Milson (16)

THERE'S NOTHING YOU CANNOT DO

There's nothing to fear - you're as good as the best,
As strong as the mightiest too.
You can win in every battle or test;
For there's no one just like you.
There's only one you in the world today;
So nobody else, you see,
Can do your work in as fine a way:
You're the only you there'll be!
So face the world, and all life is yours
To conquer and love and live:
And you'll find the happiness that endures
In just the measure you give;
There's nothing too good for you to possess,
Nor heights where you cannot go:
Your power is more than belief or guess –
It is something you have to know.
There is nothing to fear - you can and you will.
For you are the invincible you.
Set your foot on the highest hill –
There's nothing you cannot do.

Zak Templeton (15)

WHICH WEREN'T TRUE

They told us that we'd win victory
They told us that we'd be okay
They told us many things
Which weren't true

No one will get hurt
No one will die

I remember the first time we got there
How excited we all were
Me and my best friend Rob, he died the very first day
He never stood a chance

All the blood, guts and gore
Soldier's arms and legs on the floor
It was horrific
But still they told us that we'd be okay

Many died and I was lucky to be alive
But some parts of my body weren't
I now have no legs and only left with one arm
I can never cuddle nor hold soft hands and have lost all my charm

They lied to us
They told us that we'd win victory
They told us that we'd be okay
They told us many things
Which weren't true

Ambrin Ahmed

HATE

Hate is a bullet in your heart
Hate is the colour black
It tastes like a sour berry
Hate smells like a rotten body not preserved
Hate shows you a self portrait of yourself
Laughing cruelly as your best friend gets beaten up
It sounds like a blood curling scream
Hate!

Adran Remedios (10)

4

AUTUMN LEAVES

Leaves fall off the trees,
cold appears. Hot soup
running down my mouth,
a hot water bottle healing
my tummy.

I hear the leaves moaning
about the cold weather.
Ding-dong goes my door,
'Trick or treat?' I hear.

The wind drags me out the door,
I finally have freedom
to this world. Leaves on
the ground brightly coloured
like a rainbow, rain shattering
down my window.

Hanna Lili Rice-Smyth

THE WORLD OF ODDITIES

When the fish lived on land and the men lived in the sea,
The caterpillars ate chips and the women ate grass.

The meat eating dinosaurs were vegetarian and the herbivores ate meat,
When the bees made cheese and voles sold shoals of fish.

Oh, a man read a book that was closed and a paralysed woman ran away,
Oh, how I made cake that came out as a snake.

I wrote you a poem that you said was nice, when you had no voice.
And don't forget those fleas that keep boys in their beds.

And male moles that shovelled coal to keep their houses cold,
If you find this hard to believe, ask the blind bat he saw it too.

Frazer Callum Cansfield (11)

FIRST KISS OR WORST KISS?

Why do most people think,
That having your 'first kiss'
Is an amazing experience,
That nobody wants to miss?
The people who can't wait,
This poem is for those,
Here is what it's really like,
This is how it goes:
You're walking hand in hand,
Down a moon-lit street,
First your heads touch,
Then your eyes meet.
Soon you move closer,
Noses millimetres apart,
Then press your lips together,
And 'snog' with all your heart.
Soon after that,
The tongue begins to lick,
You expect to feel true love,
All you feel is sick!
Think of all the germs,
That lay inside a gum,
What illness you could catch,
Kissing is so dumb.
I really hate to spoil,
Your moment of romance,
But why not do something cleaner,
Like lovingly cuddle or dance?
I'm not being deliberately childish,
I'm just thinking realistically;
Imagine how disgusting,
Saliva flavour could be.
Maybe your breath might stink,
Revoltingly of cheese,
What if you need to burp,
Or even worse – sneeze?
If you're going to completely ignore me,
And let this information go to waste,
Then when you have your first kiss,
Please remember mouthwash, a toothbrush and paste!

Izzy Saint (11)

MY BROTHER TOM

I have a brother called Tom.
He goes off like a bomb.
He runs round and round
And jumps up and down
I don't know what to do
with my brother Tom.

He will be six soon.
He's got a birthday in June
A party he will have
because he's not at all bad.
He's my brother Tom.

I'll play him a tune
for his birthday in June
He'll have lots of toys
That are made for boys
With chocolates and sweets
And lots of treats
He'll have a ball because he'll eat them all.
That's my brother Tom.

He torments our cat, fancy that,
She hides out of sight, until it is night,
when Tom goes to bed she gets up instead, because it is quiet, 'cause Toms' such a riot,
That's my brother Tom.

Lauren Pattinson (10)

THE SUN

As the sun kicks the moon to the bay of the world gently,
A new day, a new opportunity,
Then me, as you see, am flying in my jet pack ready to explore,
Taking a piece of each planet, a taste of each place,
Now I'm back home wondering if I'll see them again.

Hiba Nur Mahmood (7)

THE HORSE FROM HELL

Have you ever seen the face
of a pony or mare
when the sun is shining bright?

It seems no harm
could be dealt by a horse,
by the gentle day, in light.

But there is one exception
you should be warned,
who rides by the wind of night . . .

Sometimes called the Dark Stallion, sometimes Terror Hooves,
or even the Kelpie,
Silently does it move.

Many myths hath been told,
of the treacherous beast,
from the Scottish Highlands,
to the islands of Crete.

Try not to meet it,
or even to see it,
for it dons a deceptive disguise,

If you fall victim
to the creature alone,
you'll turn slave to its evil eyes.

Those unlucky enough
to know of its curse
may not live to tell the tale,

For once it is mounted,
it will ride away
to a river where tortured souls wail.

For your precious life,
please never go out,
on a night when all seems well -

Because you never know
what hides in the trees,
It could be the Horse from Hell.

Saskia Cornish (12)

CALL ME WHAT YOU WANT, I DON'T GIVE A DAMN

I'm being me, cos that's who I am
I'm not gonna be herded in,
I'm not going to follow the sheep
Ain't no sheepdog gonna fence me in.
I'm shedding those feeble grey feathers,
I'm becoming the great white swan.

I'm an emo?
I'm a goth?
I'm a rebel?
I'm a punk?
I'm a rocker?
I'm a hippy?
I'm a protester?
I'm a questioner?
I'm a listener?
I'm an artist?
I'm intelligent?
I'm a pagan?
I'm a satanist?
I'm a witch?
I'm a lesbian?
I'm bisexual?
I'm straight?
I'm an animal, I'm a human.
I am who I am
I know what I want
I fight for my freedom
Don't be so stereotypical!

Call me what you want,
I don't give a damn.
You don't like me,
I don't care.
I am me,
You are you.
You don't know me
Please . . . tell me something new.

Abagail Jayne Price

HAPPINESS

Happiness is like lying in the sun on a sizzling summer's day.
Happiness is like a big fluffy jumper, keeping you warm on a cold winter's morning with the snow falling to the iced ground.
Happiness smells like a big ripe apple, ruby red sometimes deep green.
Happiness sounds like people at the circus, laughing and cheering while the clowns are fooling around.
Happiness tastes like a big mouth-watering bar of creamy chocolate melting sweetly in your mouth.
Happiness is like hot bubbling cheese on a perfectly browned piece of toast.
Happiness feels like the wind blowing gently through the trees.
Happiness is the best feeling in the world.

Harlan Nicholas (9)

MEN

Men are sly snakes,
wandering weeds, popping up
when you turn your back.
Men are nature's mistakes.

Men are grumpy gnomes,
they just sit there
a heart of stone.
Men are a waste of space.

Men are moaning mould,
annoying, arrogant
the storm cloud on a sunny day.
Men are the uninvited guests.

Men are the menacing magpies,
the ravens on the grave
disguising all their lies,
behind their feathery face.

Charlie Mason (13)

LIFELESS

Its limbs attached to thread,
Its head drooping,
With every pull it jerks,
With no choice,
If only it could pull,
Break the rope,
And never look back,
With cracks on its skin and on its shiny face,
He glares into the mirror and turns in disgrace,
A life with no freedom,
A child with no mother,
He looks at the puppeteer and cries with a shudder.

Georgia Langham (12)

JOURNEY TO YEAR SEVEN

Where would I go?
Who would I meet?
The questions whirled round in my head,
So I couldn't get to sleep when I went to bed
Everyone kept saying, 'Don't worry, you'll be fine!'
But the way they said it made it sound like a lie
The summer holidays
Flew past,
The day was getting nearer,
Very fast
Soon, the morning came
I still felt nervous but it wasn't the same
Where would I go?
Who would I meet?
The questions whirled round in my head.

Ruby McGrath (11)

A FRIEND

A smile turns into a laugh
Night turns into day
My life changed forever
And I never got a say

I wish you could see,
The way that you've changed me
I've known you forever,
Always there for me to see

Growing up with you,
Since the age of two
My friend who saw you,
Her banana you took to chew

Chewing through the wires,
To the speakers they were
Sound no longer heard
After

To some you were a rabbit
But to me
A friend,
Is all I see.

Katy Briant

OWL TWO BLUE

A long, long time ago, there was an owl, two owls, red owls, blue owls!
But there was one owl called Owl Two Blue: (TB)
Owl TB went to the zoo in someone's shoe!
Owl TB went to a party, the party was blue!
And there were two owls there and so that meant
Owl Two Blue!

Jorja Marshall (8)

OUT THERE

As I gaze up at the stars,
I wonder what's out there.
Would it be a dream,
Or could it be a nightmare?

And as I stand here,
On a planet so small.
I close my eyes,
And hear the stars call.

I close my eyes,
And drift through the darkness.
Now the planets are passing me,
And I end up in nothingness.

I feel so alone,
I have no one to guide me.
I feel so scared,
I have nothing to see.

I focus on what I love,
I focus with all my might.
My friends, my home, my life,
And suddenly I see a light.

I go to the light,
It is the thing to guide me.
The one thing I need,
It's the one thing I can see.

I see everything I love,
All the things I long for.
I open my eyes and I am back,
I have shown weakness the door.

Cameron Dunk (12)

JOHN'S MARVELLOUS MEDICINE

So give me some pencil lead and an old rusty bat.
Give me tails and a big fat cat.
And some nails.
And some snails.
And some old beds.
And some old rusty pegs.
And a big tap.
And an old cap.
Each with a sweet smell.
And a yuck taste as well.
Will she go pop?
Will she go plop?
Will she go bang?
Will she go ka-chang?
Oh Grandma, if only you knew what I have in store for you.

John Robertson

MY OWN PERSON

I am my own person,
Anyone can agree,
Nothing will change me,
Unlike the leaves of a tree.
I am my own person,
I'll think what I please,
I am not the kind,
Who would bully or tease.
I am my own person,
But I must plea,
That you like me for who I am,
Not for who you want me to be!

Zoe Nix (13)

THE NIGHTMARE

The dim room, in which I was now sitting, was coated in a dark cloud of deep doom,

The candles quivered and sent a shiver running down my spine,

I looked back and realised attack was nowhere to be near,

For there, in front of me, sat he, the skeleton of fear,

As the thought bored into me, my face turned ghostly white,

Therefore it did, illuminate the whole, dark, scary night,

A pale, bright beam of silvery moonlight, caught him in the face,

It danced around, until at last, it left without a trace,

But that wasn't all, because straight after, the ancient skull just came to life,

A withered hand, with withered skin, picked up a bloody knife,

A bellow of laughter, rang in my ears, and the shadowy face faced mine,

The knife was raised above my head, so I let myself just cry,

I closed my eyes tight, tight as I could, preparing for the blow,

What happened next, what happened next, I really do not know,

Suddenly my eyes blinked open, my face puffy and red,

All I knew right then was that, I was sitting on my bed,

I looked around in disbelief, was I going mad?

A nightmare had settled into my head, which in fact was very bad,

Never again, will I eat curry and rice,

This nightmare had happened already twice,

And of course, for sure, in case of school dinners,

I'll take a packed lunch, which will make me much thinner!

Anna Grube

SMILES

I always had a room full of piles,
inside are a million smiles.
I never miss a glorious page,
so I don't trigger my rage.
All those loving days watching them grow,
I may be thinking they'll turn low.
I should never repeat this horrid thought,
well maybe that's because that's what I ought.
Never-ending smiles,
are like weary miles.
This is why I love smiles.

Thajrin Ahmed (10)

TEARS ROLL DOWN

The tears rolled down and stained my face
My pain breaking my heart and faith
As I looked out the window and wished it was him
My brain knew I was just kidding

He had left me this morning
And told me it was over
I had run after him and begged him to stay
But my plea was unheard and he went on his way

He had met someone new
Someone better than me;
She had blue eyes and blonde hair
But why leave me; even I am beautiful and fair

I guess I wasn't enough
He was probably bored
But I loved him from my heart and soul
And now my world is a big black hole.

The tears rolled down and stained my face
I still wait for him with all my faith
I look out the window even now
My brain still forces me to walk away
But he shall be mine one day . . .

Nabeeda Bakali (16)

16

THE WAVES

The waves crash beneath me,
The creamy foam tickles my feet,
I look out to sea and spot an endless glimmer of blue,
In which the fish rule the world.
People are on the beach like measurements on a ruler,
Suncream and sunglasses swamp the sand,
I spot boats sailing silently,
And I dive into the mysterious depths.
The further I go, the more I discover,
Crabs and small fish eat at the algae,
Large groups of fish circle me,
Huge fish swim past me without a care.
The water sparkles like blue gold,
A rainbow of corals surrounds me,
Sea horses cling to thin green branches,
Puffer fish glide past me with curiosity.
I kick my feet and swim further,
The water becomes murky and unclear,
I see a large dark shadow in front,
And as I swim forward I see a shipwreck.
Nothing could compare to its size,
Its green and brown surface fills me with curious excitement,
However something tells me not to enter,
Something niggling at the back of my mind.
The fish flee, the water is silent,
Everything freezes, I cannot move,
I stare into the opening,
And all I can do is gasp in amazement.
A huge shark appears, not just grand but terrifying,
I stay completely still, not even breathing,
It stares in my direction, with beady eyes,
Then with a flash, clasps a fish right next to me.
It swims off with pride,
A memory I will never forget,
How fast it was, how strong,
That shark is the king of the ocean.

Amy Morris (13)

RAINDROP

Cold, watery, running dew
Faster than the lion, faster than you
Drip . . . Drip . . . Drip . . . Drop . . .
It can't stop, oh it really can't stop
Lighter than a feather that holds up our love
Taller than the clouds we see up above
Shining beneath us is the pot of gold
With secrets to be told and treasure to hold
It's a matter of time not a matter of speech
Things may grow, things may know
At the end of the window a red tape lies
Once I'm across it, I say *away* with those lies
I am nearly there, what am I now?
For I am the race-winning raindrop
Splish . . . Splash . . . Splosh . . . Sploosh . . .

Lucia Henry (12)

STATUE

A stone tear falls from the ancient mermaid's diamond eye that sparkles in the moonlight,
She stands alone in the centre of the garden,
Waiting for a friend,

She begins to rust in rain,
She begins to fade in the sun,
The wind is now blowing hard,
It started as a gentle breeze,
But now it's way too strong for her,

She starts to fall to the floor but the gnomes refuse to help,
And now it's too late anyway,
She crashes down to the stone brick path where weeds begin to sprout,
Fallen to a hundred pieces scattered all around,

However when you look out to the garden, out by where she stood,
You'll see her still rusting,
Still fading,
And her eye still sparkling.

Michelle Platten (12)

THE GUARDIAN

Cry for me sometimes at night,
Hold your cold pillow tight,
Go to sleep thinking of me
And live another day.
Leave footsteps in the sand,
Go places filled with memories and I will follow you.
You write my name in blood,
Scream my name in tears,
It's too late for me but not for you,
So live your life and breathe the air and I will follow you.
I will guide you through, I will follow you.
From up above or down below, I will stay with you
With memories so full of life and smiles that never fade.

Leave me one last gift.
Live your life and breathe the air
Clear your thoughts of all despair
And live forever more.
Lost in love and filled with pain
But you will follow through.
Through long lost roads and old closed doors.
I will soon find you.
When you used to look into my eyes,
I knew you loved me first sight.
I knew your last words never lied
And I knew our love was right.

'I love you' flew from your lips,
Then came a passionate kiss
I knew it was love from the start,
And now you're gone,
Nothing has changed
I know I will never feel this way again.
No matter who comes to my door,
Singing songs of true love,
I know they're nothing true,
That's why I fell in love with you.
I will follow you.
You want me back.
But it's too late for that.
So live another day.

Courteney Lee Hill (15)

JUST LIKE ME!

Just like the sun,
I will shine bright until each day is done,

Just like the moon,
I will glisten and bloom,

Just like the sea,
My existence will never end,

Just like the sand,
I'll forever be tough,

Just like the earth,
I will never stand still,

Just like a flower,
I will always grow,

Just like a baby,
I will always trust

Just like the wise,
I'll never forget,

Just like love,
I'm willing to be hurt,

Just like hate,
I'll always be strong,

Just like fame,
I'll take a risk,

Just like you,
I'll fall for that one kiss

Just like me,
My morals will never change.

Chynna Purdy

DARKNESS

Darkness, utter darkness, pitch-black sky,
No light in the never-ending pathway of nature,
No sound but trees whispering amongst themselves,
A sound so scarce it almost goes unnoticeable,
A slight dampness about the air sends a lump towards the back of my throat,
I'm all alone, so alone, nowhere to go,

Someone's listening to me,
Tip-tap, tip-tap, tip-tap
Someone's following me,
Tip-tap, tip-tap, tip-tap
Someone's watching me,
I can see someone there!
I'm not alone, not alone, never alone,

I can see a figure before me,
A man so young yet so fragile,
Such pale skin, almost...... ghost like,
Where's he gone?
He was just there? Gone,
I'm alone again. So alone, nowhere to go,

I'm starting to panic now,
Sweat dripping from my flesh,
There's no one here,
Nowhere to go,
Nothing at all,
Only me and Darkness.

Richard Paul (16)

SUMMER

The sun shines ever so bright,
Gleaming on the wonderful sites.
Ice cream dribbles down my hand,
My shoes get in a lot of sand.
The beautiful flowers gleaming in the sun,
They remind me of a glazed hot cross bun.
The glass is a beautiful glossy green,
Just like the Queen's garden in my dream.
The crystal blue sea shimmers,
Soft to the touch so that I don't quiver.
The silky feeling on my body,
The shells beneath are the colour of my ice lolly.
There are lots of parties and slumbers,
This is what makes it *summer!*

Tyra Miller (12)

WARS WITH THE WORLD

W hen you're stuck in the hated wars,
A nger bubbling in you.
R age with no cause,
S inking into your mind is voodoo.

W hether or not you're fighting,
I n the trenches you can feel the sadness.
T he speed of the bullet is like lightning,
H ow can you stand this madness?

T here is no feeling but melancholy,
H urt and stressed, you feel so lonely,
E ven the dead fill you with jealousy.

W hy am I here, this is horrible
O h why, oh why did I come?
R eally confused, this is sorrowful,
L uck will only see me the sun.
D on't, oh please don't come to the wars.

Luc Sinnadurai (12)

THE ANGEL OF DARKNESS

The Angel of Darkness,
Has spread her wings,
No face shall smile,
No song we shall sing.

The shadows are happy,
Laughing is forbidden,
The flowers are wilting,
The sun is hidden.

The playgrounds are empty,
The school is closed,
'Maybe I've won this time,' the Angel supposed.

The Earth did battle,
But the angel won,
She cast a shadow,
That killed the sun.

When the Angel died,
Back the sun came,
But there will always be something,
That will never be the same.

Molly Millar (10)

RACISM

Are you blind?
Can't you see beneath the skin you're no different from me?
It's been happening since before I was born, you just carry it on and it makes me yawn.
But sometimes when you're racist to me I get so angry I can't see clearly.
I'm sick to death of what everyone says, all day it's the same.
Are you blind?
Can't you see beneath the skin you're no different from me?

Ben Lewis (13)

THE LIE

Black and white, we're *all* the same,
Racism is nothing but a pain,
It used to be much worse,
The blacks were *cursed,*
They had no time for thought,
Because they were always bought.

Slavery *never* stops,
I feel like I'm going to drop,
I put out a whimpered cry,
Because I know I am going to *die,*
They said it was good,
But it was a *lie!*

Jack Walsh (13)

POETRY RIVALS

I know I'm going to die
As I wait my turn, I'm starting to cry
I take a hopeless sigh
Knowing I'm going to die.

As I loom over the blistering, shiny sea
I wonder why this is happening to me
I want to wake up to food and a home
With my family, but now I'm all alone.

Oh no, he's coming over with his beef
Not food. I take a look, he's kissing he's teeth
You're no bigger than me
But I want to sting him like a bee.

Bang, pow, boom I hear from the other room
That could be my mate or someone I hate
But no one deserves that
I want to hit him with a bat . . .

Jack Allen (13)

POETRY RIVALS

What's with all the hate?
Why can't blacks be with whites, whites with Asians
We are not any different, we are all the same inside,
Who started this hate and thinking people are better than each other?

Black is white
Stop pulling each other down
What's wrong with the world people living like they are on top
I think we should just stop

Why you at me with all this beef
What you doing kissing your teeth
You're no bigger than me
It's like I'm being squished like a bee .

Corey Parkin

JUSTICE

I feel like it's unfair, I wasn't even there
A sea of white faces judging, sitting, scared
It wasn't me I plead, words they don't believe
Not only am I black, I'm young and wear a cap

They say it was assault, I say it's not my fault
The victim said I match, he remembered a hoody and a cap
Just because I can rhyme doesn't mean I did the crime
Just because I can rap doesn't mean I gave him a slap

Then it occurred to me, I had an alibi
They state the time, it was around 4.45
I was in Burger King getting a large fries
Check the cameras 'cause the camera never lies

Now I'm free and the perpetrator is caught
He was a white, older man; not what they thought!

Matteo Wright-Jarrard

WAR GAME

People often go to have fun,
Where each has a tacky laser gun.
After all it's only one harmless game,
Hoping to credit a little friendship fame.

Many struggle with the luminous vest,
Wishing their score to be the best.
Not too dissimilar from the reality of war,
However it involves a lot less gore.

Countdown begins as they enter the scene,
With everyone becoming very keen.
Five, four, three, two, one *go!*
Now is the time to lie low.

You rise quickly but get shot,
Sorry but this will happen a lot.
Don't worry your light will flicker back on,
But if it were real your soul would be gone.

In the army you would immediately be armed,
Which might leave a few feeling totally alarmed.
Off you go to do some training,
Although it feels more like a caning.

Delving straight into the thick of it,
You are anxious to get a good hit.
Ignoring the feeling of being a witch,
After pressing the death-defying switch.

Lying on the blood-soaked ground,
Struggling to think as your head pounds.
Trying to grasp why it came to this,
When life before was so bliss.

So I'm sorry if you think I am being lame,
Because war is not like this pathetic little game.
War really is a completely different case,
So if you're thinking about joining head back to base.

Elsa Merrett (14)

EVOLUTION AND HUMAN NATURE

South-east came the rock
All because I stole his kill
'Argh, argh' a two-footed gorilla roared
So I hid in my cave
Fierce winds raged and clouds threw bolts
Still no food
With nothing but a pointy stick
Hungry

Down in the street, market stalls came to life
With just a few denarii
I had no choice
Grabbed and ran past blurry faces
Almost past the town of villas
'Siste! Siste!' a fat man yelled
As an arrow hit my foot
Hurt

The doctor said he'd cut my leg
The pain was gone
1:00
The bakery would've been open
I edged through the door with a few shillings
Loaf of bread
Eyes glued, saliva dripped
Grabbed and ran past blurring cars
'Stop that man!' a cockney ran
As a bullet pierced the air and skin
Left, right, right, left
Hidden with cargo
Escaped

Towering giants reached the sky
Everything turned so hi-fi
A hospital!
Bandaged and the bleeding stopped
Then a motor churned in my stomach
And drove me towards a sushi restaurant
The motor rested
A bill he asked, but to thin air
'Yamete yamete' words were mumbled
But it only took one bomb
Dead

Vignesh Nallathambi

27

WHERE THEM GIRLS AT?
(This is to be read in a fast tempo)

We live in a world where girls are no longer girls.
Where every day, I find myself one click away
From a girl who's breasts are angled down and out
And whose face is twisted into a duck pout
And I can feel myself wanting to shout.
Hey lady I don't mean to hate
But I feel like you may want me to translate
And state, so just think and wait
Bring it back from the complexities of the English tongue
Filled with words, verbs
Whilst you sit in the suburbs
Waiting for what you feel is your turn.
To be big, to be huge
But not too huge 'cause no one likes a fatty,
No one hires a fatty,
No one wants to see a fatty on their screen.
We want tall, we want lean,
We want thin.
We want a girl to be able to move her lips
But mute the content in-between.
We are a nation obsessed
With how a woman is dressed,
Surgically enhance their breasts,
Until there's nothing left.
Plastic.
Like a Barbie doll.
Obsessing and stressing about our rolls,
The role we are playing,
We are designed to entertain.
Where a woman's face overpowers her brain,
Overpowers what she's actually saying.
And for what?
To gain the attention she yearns for,
She earns for,
She learns for.
Pulling and crying over every last flaw.
Impossible creatures dance on her screen,
Whilst her hands flick through a magazine,
Portraying the idea of a perfect teen.

So she lies there preening,
I can hear myself screaming,
Yelling at the top of my lungs,
For this to stop.
Please stop.

Alex Beighton (16)

MY SPRING STORY

As the flowers go bright,
They need water and light,
When the flower starts to grow,
Stand back and think wow,
Easter is also in spring,
I can't wait to hear the Easter bunny sing,
We get chocolate eggs,
Sweets and treats,
For dinner we have fish, wine and meats,
But the main thing is the Easter show,
I've got tickets for the front row,
The play was about a rabbit that could sew,
The trees long,
The wind whistles a song,
Children have lots of fun,
As they play and run,
With a friend,
Till the end.

Jodie Rebecca Galley (8)

SISTER BLISTER

Sister blister
Twins for ever
Leila Talia
Break up never

Funny future
Pulling faces
Fight and squabble
No embraces

Getting up and
Falling down
Special hugs
An upset frown

Shocking surprises
Silly jokes
Play all day
Pinch and poke

Sister blister
Laugh and giggle
Hiding seeking
Wormy wiggle

Sister blister
I don't care
We'll be together
Secret share.

Talia Issacharoff (8)

HOW DOES IT END?

How does it end?
How does it stop?
So many theories,
But which one's the top?
A nuclear war?
The west or the south?
A terrible plague?
All comes from the mouth.
Will the world overflow?
Or will it decay?
Some say it's tomorrow,
But what if today?
Global warming,
Is my fairest concern.
The animals and trees,
Their death it has earned.
A volcano exploding?
An asteroid or space?
Which end does this poor,
Little world have to face?
As I spin my globe,
My mind goes to wonder,
How will the world end?
Which crisis it's under?

Jenny-Aimee Nzabandora (13)

HOW LUCKY AM I?

The sky was passion fruit purple and midnight black,
Like an enormous bruise stuck in the seemingly endless blue sky.
Time was passing from this wondrous world,
Tick tock, tick tock
And for the first time I decided to stop, to wait, to think, to understand.
So I did . . .

Around the world there are so many people,
They are all different, unique, diverse and ambitious.
Some so fortunate with money, riches and happiness
Some so adverse, with nothing
Africa, Asia, South and North America,
Full of people who deserve more than poverty
They need a full heart to fill in the emptiness of their lives.

The pain of watching the weak,
So bony, so innocent, brings endless tears to my eyes.
The misery of hearing screeches from starving children,
It makes me want to rip my ears off just to stop the agony.

How lucky am I
To have clothes, food, shelter and basic healthcare to save me when in danger?
People with such privileges don't understand how lucky they are.
But the unprivileged, they are naked . . .
No protection, no aid.

Hope is the only thing they feed on.
Help is the only thing they crave for.
And relief is the only thing they can only dream of.

However one day
The day when the sun will defeat the purple-black bruises
Will be the day when all the grief escapes
A great triumph to human kind!
For now I walk off from this trance
I can only wish for the best of both worlds.

Mehnaz Ahmed (14)

FIREWORKS

Fireworks in the pitch-black sky
Yellow, blue and pink
Gleaming in the sky
Like rockets launching up into space
While making a big *s-c-r-e-a-m!*
Bang! Boom! Bash! In a frightening way
They erupt like bombs *exploding* in the air
But wow! It's so *a-m-a-z-i-n-g*
And they're as fast as *l-i-g-h-t-n-i-n-g*
They make me scared and make me JUMP!

Zachary Morrison (8)

RACISM

Is ignorance becoming a race?
Black, white and Asian
They all have a different face.
I simply can't keep up the pace.

Discrimination, immigration
Everyone   starting some sort of segregation, racism in the air
Why can't we all just grow a pair?

Every time I hear knife crime
I hear the same constant rhyme
Another black person doing hard time.

Are you really scared of what's in sight?
Because I think it's just a stereo type
So next time think right.

Dylan Norford (13)

THE TRAGEDY OF THE THIRD BATTLE

Two knights of separate kingdoms
Two knights of similar skill
Prepared to have a skirmish
Each fighting for the kill
Sir Harten fought for honour
Sir Casket fought for grace
But both would see the outcome
Of this wretched murder race

The battle symbols came together,
The duel had begun.
The watchers shrieked with terror
They had never seen such fun
As when the silver swords clashed and cut
Glinting in the sun

A hasty swoop
A startled gasp
One held the other in his grasp
The blood-stained sword
Shone a dazzling red
As Harten raised his sword, his adversary said:

'I beg you, do not kill me
I'm after a prize tonight
I wish to shed your own red blood
See it twinkle in the light,
I want the sparkles in your eyes
To dull and dim and fade
I want the everlasting honour
Of knowing you are slayed!'

Alas, it seemed as if the knight
Would surely die that day
This being the third battle
The two had now exchanged

Luck and fate and chance
Had so far kept the two alive
However it appeared as though
Only one man would survive

Harten's outstretched hand wavered in the light
With a clang his weapon fell to the dust
And Casket was the winner
Of this corrupted fight

34

Then it seemed a privilege
But soon regret was found
And late one bitter afternoon
He stood by the river, and frowned;
And by the light of the ghostly moon
He then and there was drowned.

Annabelle Fuller (11)

TO WIN IS MY DREAM

Training for years with the dream to be a winner
Performance, pressure, power, pleasure
Loving the feeling of being the best in the world
Friends and rivals fighting for gold.

Straining, sweating, suspense.
Minutes, seconds, ticking by
Cameras watching every move
 Every twitch captured forever
Feeling the pain but carrying on
Feeling the pain but never giving up
Fear of loosing, fear of failing
Fear of letting down a nation

National flags dancing in the breeze
Multi-coloured costumes parading past
Cheering, clapping crowds
Young to old wanting to see it

Some were lucky and got tickets,
Others disappointed and didn't make it
But TV will make you feel you're there
With the Olympic dream and flame to share

I love the Olympics and I'm sure you do too
Come to London and be part of it too
2012 is the year it's here
The ultimate gold
One winner, one gold
To win is my dream!

Clara Morrison (10)

SNOW

Pure white snow falls as a salt-shaker's sprinkles,
Coating the charcoal streets of Epsom,
An unblemished layer of chalky, sugar icing,
Is now tarnished by naïve, wandering citizens,
Footsteps crunch the icing and leave unflattering grey stains in their wake,
The soft, damp scoops are crafted into frosty spheres and hurled at unsuspecting residents.

Vehicles trundle along cautiously, tearing through the perfect wintry blanket,
Then the rain falls, thousands of teardrops splattering down,
Falling in tonnes, merciless to the powdery sheet.

The smooth white cotton is pummelled into mush,
And trickles away in defeat, the murky sludge squelching into nothing.

And Epsom is dreary and lifeless again,
With nothing but drizzle to remember the elegant spread,
As we wait for its stunning re-appearance next year.

Maryam Adil (15)

BRIGHTEST STAR

(This poem is in memory of one of my friends, Leonie Jo Nice, who sadly passed away a couple of months ago and I miss her dearly.)

You are our sun
The brightest star in the sky
I miss you so much
You didn't even say bye
You were so pretty, so nice, so kind
You was really talented
And had every right to shine
Rest in peace
Leonie Jo Nice
You're in a better place now
You're in paradise.

India Davies (12)

THE BEAUTIFUL GREY

It is grey.
Some call it bleak.
But so what if the clouds do not seek attention?
Unlike the sun.
Shining painfully and catching eyes.
But still, the sun is spoken of positively,
Even once we had penetrated its disguise.

Beauty in grey is bypassed.
It does not demand you
And so it is not noticed.
Consider if you will, the exciting, enigmatic mist
Which enhances all we see;
Illuminating the blue of the sky
And making our trees appear more green.

'And the weather today
Will unfortunately be grey.'
Dark shadows invade our canvas,
Meticulously painted to be perfect.
These clouds give us clear, sparkling jewels
But we only complain,
To the extent that we have learnt to dread their name.

Open your mind to open your heart,
And let the grey touch you, taint you,
Leave their imprint.
The grey are ambiguous,
Interpret them as you like
But do not ignore them.
Appreciate them and the grey shall appreciate you,
Because those who appreciate grey,
Oh, there are so few.

Rachael Palmer (17)

THE MONSTER

I'd rather have acne scars
and tobacco tar
mutilating the contours of my face,
lapping at my lungs;
than undulations
across my skull
where your tiara clung
or the taste
of blood against my teeth,
from the thousand times
that you held your
tongue.

Claire Smith (15)

LILLY FARM

Lilly farm, that's where we'll be . . .
On a fresh spring's morning, or a midsummer's lunch,
The warming winter dinner, even eleven o'clock brunch,
At Lilly farm it all takes place,
And as for sorrow, there isn't a trace.
Lilly farm, that's where we'll be.

Lilly farm is a comforting home,
Where no person is sad or alone,
The dancing flames of the fire they burn,
And the wisdom and kindness from which they will learn,
The art of the love, the caring and sharing.
Lilly farm, that's where we'll be.

So now I have proved this point to you,
Let's go to Lilly farm for a Joyce-like toot.
Lilly farm, that's where we'll be.

Daisie Hadley (10)

HOLOCAUST

War! War! Oh dreaded war!
In the fields of death and gore!
What stains the foundations of life itself-
Will have left a book on the history shelf.

Some remember it clearly,
Some not so well.
Some try to forget this troubling Hell.

Nonetheless -
What can be forgotten,
Alas,
Will have already happened,
And those who were
Fighting and present,
Will think of it
Not so pleasant.

Six worrisome years of war,
In the fields of death and gore.
Number of countries affected:
Totals one-o-four.

Mass murders, sullen soldiers,
Tedious time in trenches.
Horrid holocaust, ghastly guns,
And in soldiers' boots were roaches.

The infamous 'Arbeit macht frei',
Famous for its mocking lie.
Gateway to death and torture.
To bloodshed tears and slaughter.

Concentration. Limitation,
To what freedom provides.
Desperation. Needing salvation,
From this crazy, mad world.

 Caged like animals in the zoo.
What the devil did this to you?
What fearful being? What fearful monstrosity?
The cause of all this strife and atrocity.

War! War! Oh dreaded war!
In the fields of death and gore.
It is gone. It is done. 1945.
But still there are those who could not survive.

Bayan Fadlalla (13)

A RAINBOW IN THE SKY

A rainbow in the sky, something to see before you die
The colours are so bright and shine in pure daylight

Red is a deep, dark colour
The one that you will take
If you are a really good lover

A rainbow in the sky, something to see before you die
Colours full of bliss, something that you can't miss

Orange is so pretty
It's the colour of a city

A rainbow in the sky something, to see before you die
It's formed by the rain in the heavens blue
And the rays of the sunshine too

Yellow is so mellow
The colour you think of in summer warm weather

A rainbow in the sky, something to see before you die
It's beautiful when you see it
And you wish that you could be it

Multicolour lovers look up and discover
Red, orange, yellow, green
This is the happiest I have ever been

A rainbow in the sky
Something to see before you die
But it will soon fade away
And the sky will be ash grey.

Zaquira Lawson-Cos (12)

TITANIC

Bright coloured fireworks filled the night skies,
Accompanied with the sound of faint, distant cries.
Mothers and children were the first to be placed on the boats
While the men kept on screaming, fighting, at each other's throats.
The waves of the sea started to fill up the large ship
But mostly at the bottom end, causing it to tip.
The boats were all full then and there was nowhere to go
So the ones left behind must sink down below.
And while all this chaos happened, the survivors just stared,
No one caring for those who were drowning and scared.
Fifteen hundred people had died from the bone-chilling cold
None getting the chance to live on, to grow old.
In 1912, the greatest ship was sent out to sea.
Unsinkable they had claimed, well they could've fooled me.
On the 14th April, a century ago, erupted great panic
Because of a voyage to America, on the great ship Titanic.

Bethany Nicholls (15)

POLICE CHASE

Sirens screaming
Lights flashing
Helicopter's searchlight beaming
Rain pouring
Tyres splashing
Engines roaring
Cars speeding
Villains leading
Back-up needed
Tyres skid
Crash! Bang!
Villains down
Police arrest.

Charlotte Kite

HOPE, FAITH AND KINDNESS

Is it something new? Or maybe a shoe, is it something for me or an extra yummy tea?
Some string, an orange or maybe a pear but when I walked through the door the room was bare.
Nothing but boxes and of course mum and me. We've been homeless all my life, it's not nice you see.
We sleep in a warehouse and scavenge for food.
As you can imagine it doesn't put us in a very good mood.
It makes me sad, living in poverty but all I can do is pray that we'll always manage to find tea.
We'll probably live like this for the rest of our lives. Unless a miracle happens or someone is kind.
That's the problem, there's not enough kindness around.
Nobody notices us, we're not even in the background.
But I will keep faith and I will keep hope and together me and Mum will cope.

Zsuzsanna Peach Bull (11)

PEACOCK

The way the peacock flushes its feathers and wings,
It is in places or temples with bells that ping.
The feathers look like they have got eyes,
Peacocks don't eat flies.
Peacocks are true,
They have feathers that are blue.
They have beautiful feathers,
They are like leathers.
They are bright,
And have might.
They have thin legs,
They have small heads.
They beautifully flutter
I sometimes mutter
They dance in the rain
But most of the time they walk straight and don't open their mane
They are so bright
The underneath of their beaks are like white
Their feathers glisten in the sunshine.
Green and fine.
This is the peacock end!

Sangavai Punnyaseelan (8)

CROWDED ROOM

I'm in a crowded room, that's full of empty faces,
My life is falling at the edges, like the autumn leaves fall to the floor,
You were my one and only surrender, one life I could choose.
The autumn leaves are falling from their branches,
They spin and twirl till they hit the floor,
Just like our lives, they fell apart, tonight.

I'm in a crowded room, that's full of empty faces,
The season change has caused our hearts to brake,
The leaves are crunching on the floor.
It sounds just like our lives, which are left to burn.

The autumn storm has broken us again,
With leaves that just mock our lives,
We're dying on the outside.
While trying to live inside

I'm in a crowded room, that's full of empty faces,
So I guess this is, what we call the end,
Cause I can't see your faces anymore

Jessica Hardaker

FOX

Fox scurries quickly through the forest.
He sees green bushes and mini beasts.
He runs like the wind through the forest.
Then he stops.
He is finding prey.
His eyes are small as marbles.
He is a fierce furry fox.
Then he sees a chicken, then *pounces*!
The chicken is dead.
Fox now crunches and munches the chicken.
He has eaten so much that there are only bones left.
Stinky bones!

Ben William Hornby

PATCHWORK

When I hear your name
I turn from the voice who spoke it
Why?
When I hold, smell, touch objects
that used to belong to you
I'm desperately trying to remember
cling to your memory.
I feel I might die.

As I wander through life's path
I am suddenly reminded of you by the tiniest
everyday detail
My eyes demand to cry but I fight them
Why?

Was it really that long ago that you left me
not to return having never said goodbye
Why? Why didn't you say goodbye?
When I would have gladly swapped the world
to have done so to you.

I realise that my sorrow, outrage and naive nature
was just a personal patchwork of emotions to help me get by
Now when I look at that photo of us on that sunny day
with my small hand in your safe, older one
I smile
Why?
Because I still love you.

Rebecca Bailey

THE WILSONS

The Wilsons are a family of four and a dog as well
Why he's so lazy I couldn't tell
He eats almost anything
Just when he's not sleeping.

Mama Wilson cleans and cooks
She doesn't read a lot of books
When we misbehave she goes mad
She always finishes with, 'You're some lad.'

Papa Wilson is different
He hardly cooks at all
Overall he's a real nice gent
He's only good at football.

Little brother Wilson is a bit cheeky
He's not one bit geeky
He's good at a video game
But against his big brother he's totally lame.

Then there's big brother Wilson
He always has to be a champion
He's the smartest of the lot
He's a real ladies man as they all think he's hot.

So that's the Wilson family
They all have their qualities as such
They may have their problems
But they love each other so much.

Owen Wilson

SEASONS

There are four seasons,
They take place every year.
It happens all around the globe,
And makes the world superb.

Autumn is a season,
Where leaves fall off the trees.
Nature starts to slowly decrease,
Especially wasps and bees.
The leaves fall off and fly in the air,
Eventually hitting the ground.
The colours of the leaves just lie there,
Scattered all around.

Winter is a season,
Where countries go dull and cold.
The temperature decreases dramatically low,
As autumn begins to fold.
Snow eventually starts to fall,
White blizzards here and there.
The ground covers all in white,
And affects almost everywhere.

Spring is a season,
Where the leaves grow back on trees.
Nature starts all over again,
With flies and honey bees.
The snow starts to die out,
The weather and temperature increase.
The ducks and birds come back out,
As well as well as swans and geese.

Summer is a season,
Where the sky turns ocean blue.
The sunshine and temperature change again,
And sunburn tries to get you.
The sea is warm and full of people,
The air is roaring hot.
The ice cream vans appear again,
Summer has the lot.

Seasons change throughout the year,
The weather changes too.
The temperatures can go up and down,
The sky can be grey or blue.

No matter what the weather,
Or any other reasons.
This is a continuous yearly change,
And we call it; seasons.

Samuel Bateman (15)

GOING HOME

Flying in the light, blue sky,
No one can stop me when I'm this high.
Diving in and out of trees,
I can do as I please.
My feathers being ruffled by the breeze,
Here's a chance that I will seize.

I'm flying to where I'm supposed to be,
Nobody else; just happy, little me.

Heading towards the setting sun,
Who'd have thought this would be so much fun.
Not another creature in sight,
Probably all gone to rest for the night.
I could go around and fly for days,
In the warmth of the sun's huge, yellow rays.

I'm flying to where I'm supposed to be,
Nobody else, just happy, little me.

I'm nearly there I can see the land,
It's a place with sea and sand.
I'm so excited, I'm wild, I'm free,
No one could be happier than me.
I spot a rainforest just a small distance away,
The children, they're smiling, they sing as they play.

I'm finally home where I should be,
In Rio, with nobody else just happy, little me.

Jessica Saint (10)

SILENCE?

What is silence?
You can't hear it to define it
You can't see it to know it's there
You can't sniff it out
It's just hollow in the air

It creeps up on you when you're alone
It leaves when there's a crowd
It isn't quiet, it isn't loud
It's just hollow in the air
But still questioning, silence?

Bullied away from the fun
It's like the moon, stars and sun
You don't question why it's here
Without an appearance and you in a trance
Silence is free wherever it may be

You don't think what silence hears
When you ask it won't come
When you turn a back it appears
It's just hollow in the air

It's not a thing, it's not a sound
Not a movement on sky or ground
Not a person, not a place
It's just there in the space
It's just hollow in the air

But to break the silence
Shattered a million to a piece
Scattered on the marble floor
The mirror of sound

Still, what is silence?
You can't hear it to define it
You can't see it to know it's there
You can't sniff it out
It's just hollow in the air
Or is it?

Gemma Clark (12)

DEAR TEACHER

Okay look I do understand,
That poets often write something grand,
It's great, yes I can see,
But really, don't go on at me,
About it being a 'masterpiece',
'The depth to this will never cease,'
I mean, please, keep it real,
Not really such a big deal.
You think about it far too much,
Seriously don't make such a fuss,
Coz teacher you're getting out of hand,
It's only a poem about some sand.
Darlin' we've made so many notes,
That the true meaning can't connote,
I don't think poets write for school,
So please stop making poems so uncool.
And teacher, you know what?
Even I can write about a flowerpot,
So don't look into it quite so much,
You're going to lose sanity's touch,
Just leave it as it's meant to be,
A piece of art for you and me.

Ellie Turnbull

ANIMALS

Fishes swim, snakes slide,
kangaroos jump, rays glide,
penguins waddle, horses trot,
elephants stomp, camels spit a lot,
pigs oink, spiders crawl,
dogs love to play with balls,
and my daisy cat puuuurrrrrrrrs
a lot.

Chianna Ede-James (7)

JOEY: MAFIA

Tell me. Why should I help you?
You who sit here before me,
Talking about how you,
Needed the money, how this
'Way of life' felt too uncanny.
Fair enough.
So tell me, why should I spare you?
You who kneel before me,
Complaining about how you
Need your life back, how your
'Mind ain't on track'
Well then . . .
I could, I know I could spare you,
If that is what you want from me.
But, listen before you feel relief, because I
do not 'trust' you. I
do not 'pity' you.
Not at all.
Did you really think I would spare you?
Help you? No, I did not think you did.
(At his men) Look how he
trembles with fear. How he
holds back his tears.
Just get on with it,
I have no mercy.

Tanya Bass

THE LIFE OF A FIVE-YEAR-OLD CHIMNEY SWEEP

I cry and I cry, 'Help! I'm stuck!'
I hope someone will come, but no such luck.

My throat is raw, yet how many come? None.
Do they think I cry and cry for fun?

The blackened soot, it falls and completely covers me,
Like the thickest smog, it immediately smothers me.

I push and I struggle, but alas and alack,
I have to stop when there's a sickening crack.

I try to think clearly through the agonising pain,
I must be better before I'm up a chimney again.

A vision emerges through the clouds so white,
It's the rooftop where I sleep at night.

I try to work out if this is one of those dreams,
It might not be as lovely as it seems.

The sky is still blue, the sun, it still sears,
Then out of nowhere, a doctor appears.

I'm suddenly filled with dread and hate,
I start to run, but I think it's too late.

The doctor catches me and begins to shake,
How many of my bones are there left to break?

All of a sudden, I snap back to reality,
The clouds lift and I see everything with amazing clarity.

The doctor is there, same as before,
How did Master afford it? He is ever so poor.

Now that I'm better, my knees are rubbed with brine,
I'm shoved up the chimney, no time to whine.

Charlotte Barber

BUBBLES OF PHILOSOPHY . . .

In the beginning there was only light
Then from somewhere
In nowhere
A sliver of black
A tiny crack in the light.
Disturbance

From darkness, shimmering glass orbs
Floating weightlessly
Never ceasing,
Drifting though the brightness
Sparking their own miracles.
Awe

Each bubble, a thought
That grew and grew
Vast spinning emotions
Wondering and dreaming.
Imagination

Emerging from one somersaulting sphere
A shapeless shadow
A delicate body
Silhouetted against the purity.
Soul

Dancing aimlessly across peaceful heartlands
It revelled in itself
Unconsciously
The rhythmic mind taken across the luminosity
To the darkened gateway.
Blissful

Staring deep
An unfilled corner in its heart
Loneliness lingered
Tears touched the light
Transforming it into simple dimness.
Longing

Weary of the white tranquillity
Inspired by the black empty void
A pattern of thoughts made music
Enriched brilliance shining more intensely
Blinded to anyone but itself and the shadowed opening.
Realisation

Grasping the blackness, pulling it across the light
Rolling up the rest of the radiance,
Positioning a ball in the centre
Recognising no need to imagine a wonderland
Simply to become one.
Understanding

Body dissolved in planets
Eyes, the watchful moon
Breath as wind
Mind into minds
Star spheres floating
God is everything.

Dali Lemon-Morgan (13)

MARY HAD A LITTLE LAMB . . .

Mary had a little lamb,
It roamed around with glee;
When it left the house one day,
It befriended a bee.

The bee was rather smart,
So it fooled the little lamb,
The lamb was left alone,
Whilst eating tasty yam.

The lamb was feeling bored,
Along there came a fly,
The lamb felt really brave,
Whereas the fly was really shy.

Although the lamb was sleepy,
There was no bed in sight,
It had just one choice:
To follow Mary's kite.

The little lamb now changed its mind,
Instead it went to fight,
It ended up in trouble,
It didn't do what was right!

Neha Jitendra (11)

MY DEAREST DUKE OF EDINBURGH

My dearest Duke of Edinburgh, I'm just writing to say,
We loved the expedition that we did the other day,
We loved the wrong direction we set off in at the start,
Going back there two hours later was another thrilling part,
Sinking through a field of knee deep sludge, was wonderful, it's true,
We adored it when the sole was sucked clean off my leather shoe,
We loved the field of wild brown cows that were viciously angry and large,
We loved it when they mooed at us and kicked the ground to charge,
We adored our dodgy compass and our dung-brown-splattered map,
We prized the blatant uselessness for our sun cream and sun cap,
 We loved our dead dull project on the Ordnance Survey chart,
And standing in a waist deep bog we loved with all our heart,
 We loved the barbed wire fences that blocked the route we picked
And even better climbing them, to see our clothes get ripped,
We cherished being the final team to get to the campsite,
We'll ever prize the memories of that wet and windy night,
We loved the tasteless camping food; we cooked out on the grass,
We loved the plastic substitutes that replaced our plate and glass,
Even more we loved our leaking tent that soaked us through the night,
We loved our smelly morning feet: a ripped and ragged sight,
We did love being woken at a civilized 5:08,
Plus our aching feet and dead sore backs really were first rate,
We loved setting off with heavy packs, trudging up steep hills,
Gosh, our D of E adventure really *was* filled up with thrills,
We loved marching through the forests and crawling up mud slopes,
And that yummy Marmite hot cross bun did surpass my hopes,
Our hay-fever loved the waist high grass through which we gaily strode,
We loved waiting for an hour or so to be crossed over the road!
Our muddy, sweaty clothes and aching shoulders we loved too,
Just not nearly half as much as that freezing, campsite loo,
We adored our weighty rucksacks as we hurdled styles and logs,
We loved the cows, the bees, the sheep, the horses, birds and dogs,
My dearest Duke of Edinburgh, I loved my D of E,
There was just something about it that was not quite right for me,
I truly, dearly loved it: the mud, the blood, the pain,
Now I'm only left to puzzle out: why I *won't* do it again!

Philippa Louise Crundwell (14)

THE IMPORTANCE OF EDUCATION

For a bright future education is required,
Without it only regrets are acquired,
Education gives you short-term pain,
But in the end you receive long-term gain,
Education is not only about factual knowledge,
It's also about practical knowledge,
Education makes a person stand on their toes
Education helps a person destroy their foes,
If a man is educated
For the remainder of his life he'll be elated,
Education is extremely prominent
Without it you can't lead a life which is dominant,
Education is a life-sustaining material,
Without it you can't lead a life which is congenial,
Good education is gained through concentration
And leads to the path of civilisation,
Education improves your communication
Which helps build a strong relation,
Believe in yourself and use that power to become notorious
or use it correctly and become glorious,
It is a lie that you can gain knowledge,
Only at school or at a college,
You're fortunate enough to have an education
Use it wisely and don't be a humiliation.

Mohammed Ariq Rahman

THE LABYRINTH OF THE MIND

The dark, deep caves,
The recesses of your heart,
In it, slithering, a demon,
The sickest, evil part,
The demon broke free,
Entering the labyrinth of the mind,
Controlling you,
No longer kind,
Your inner demon coming through,
That is the real you.

Luke Hassett (13)

JUNE RAIN

Now that summer's here
And people leave school
Everyone smiles
The sun is their tool.

All are laughing,
All but one
June Rain looks on
Watching her foe, Sun.

Her hair gossamer
And the smile of a reptile.
The eyes of a vixen
And the aim of a missile.

Stuck in the clouds,
Hates to see joy.
Storm clouds come in seconds
She doesn't play coy.

At the first drizzle,
People don't mind.
To the havoc ahead
They're deaf, dumb and blind.

Rain starts to get heavier
There grows a dull din,
Up in the clouds,
June Rain grins.

Children of old
Of whom June Rain knows,
Begin to fret,
Their anxiety shows.

They know of June Rain
And they of her tricks.
Light showers one moment,
Flash floods the next.

Gutters are blocked
And people start to worry.
The drainpipe bursts,
Spray makes roads blurry.

Those who live up hill
Barricade their gates,
Unfortunates below
Begin to evacuate.

Cars break down in the
Middle of the road,
Soon swept on by,
Children do as their told.

As havoc engulfs the town
She once called home,
June Rain still smiles in the clouds
Alone.

She is bored now,
Feels she's done enough.
To justify her actions,
She cries, 'What doesn't kill them, makes them tough!'

'Why should I suffer?
Neither dead nor alive
When, generations later
Those I left, *thrive*!'

'I was young too once,
A child, free just to be,
Then with one lousy driver
That was ripped from me!'

'On my way to Heaven,
Something swayed!
Until I rest, I torture!'
Then she walks away.

The rain eases up,
Though it's still spitting down.
Not all is lost,
So far, no one's drowned.

'No job for girls,'
Is the reply,
When I ask to help.
(I don't bother with 'Why?')

So I sit behind the window,
Watching repairs
While June Rain drizzles down,
The very symbol of despair.

Grace Magee (12)

MY DEAR LITTLE STORY

My dear little story
Still fresh in my head.
You're on my mind,
Even when I wake up from bed.

You stay with me,
Until your life thread is spun.
And then dear little story,
You're all one.

At first you're only a cobweb,
Taking up space.
But then your ideas
Start coming at a fast pace.

Like a slow dancer,
You circle and twirl.
Giving me your adventures,
Romantic thrills.

What a dream
To fall asleep to the sound of rain,
What a dream
To walk through a field of wild flowers
All blooming and green,
What a dream
To meet the one I will love
For the rest of my life,
What a dream.

Dreams to make me smile,
And dreams to make me frown.
Dreams of beautiful stones,
Still cobwebs in my head.
Dreams of great sorrow,
Some of great dread.

Ayesha Khan (11)

THE WONDROUS POEM OF THE GODS

I pull the strings,
And make the chords,
I press the keys,
And flow the song,
The song overflows,
With love and care,
The love and care spread everywhere!

The blossomed notes surround the warm atmosphere!
The sun shines brightly and the moon smiles grandly!
The planets spin faster than ever,
Happy and glad,
The music's around,
They dance together a rock ballad!

Beautiful birds boom with beaming tweets,
Chirping their way through the harmonic sounds.
While the heartbeat,
Hums a romance tune,
And falls in love with a popstar,
Whom?

Throughout the time,
The weather has learnt to play its rhythm too.
Rain taps delightfully,
Playing the pulse of the Earth,
Tick-tock, tick-tock, tick-tock, tick-tock.
Snow arrives majestically,
Sharing its simple crinkling sound when squashed together.
Even the sorrow thunder of them all,
Bellows it shattering . . .
Bang!

The music of the Gods,
Singing gratefully,
'We are more than amazed with this rhythm, thank you.'
And I reply, proudly, but not as proud as the tunes,
'Thank you! The melody notes are too!'

Ruxandra Ilie (12)

59

MY LIFE FLIES BEFORE MY EYES

He points his gun at me and fires
My life rewinds before my eyes
And now it is expired
I am too young and not so wise
But I will pay for all my lies
I'm sorry for all the lives I took
All those countless names can fill a whole book
I wasn't right,
Nor was I fair,
And I can't fight,
Nor can I care
All those lives I took before,
But I have got to kill even more,
And this is not something I can ignore
I remember the day I met her,
I fell in love but she vanished in a blur
I thought I wasn't someone she'd prefer,
But the truth punched me in the guts
She got shot in the heart
And we were forced to fall apart
Half of me died and life had no point
I went to find that little prat,
The one that killed my loved one,
How could he do it?
That ugly rat
To kill the biggest beauty,
I had to find that little prat,
I had to do my duty
I remember how I tracked him down,
The day that we first met,
He was at home, just down town,
Watching TV, I bet,
I held him at gunpoint,
And swore at him a bit
I got annoyed so I decided to give him a little hit
He begged and cried,
Pleaded and lied,
I wouldn't leave,
It's his time to grieve
I loaded my gun,
Pointed it at him,
And fired, I've won
He fell to the floor,

Blood-stained the carpet
It didn't matter anymore,
The enemy was gone and shattered
But all that was left was pride, desire,
I liked it, I felt a new kind of fire
I decided to do it again and again
I killed many people
And took many lives
But my heart got stabbed with more and more countless knives,
I wasn't old Andrew,
I was someone new
My heart was a rotting apple,
Infected with flu
I'm going to Heaven, to see her again
Or maybe to Hell to pay for those men
Thank you dear stranger for taking my life
And saving so many others from my life-taking knife
You'll be rewarded, I know for sure
But don't make my mistakes
And that is all it takes
He points his gun at me and fires,
The bullet shoots across the room,
And finds my heart in the gloom,
Blood sprays and stains my newest suit
In the distance I hear her play the flute,
I can't feel my toes, my fingers, my head
This is how it feels to be dead . . .

Arina Bykova

LIFE SERMON

Sometimes life doesn't turn out the way you want it to
Sometimes it punches you in the stomach, then laughs at you afterwards,
Sometimes it gives you everything, then takes it all back again in one minute,
Sometimes it plays with you, and then watches you fall into its trap without a word of dispute,
Sometimes it confides in you, then goes back on every word you have ever been taught,
Sometimes it teaches you the beauty of the world, then gives you nothing but pain and hatred to remember,
Sometimes it gives you dreams to aspire to, then watches you meet the likes of disappointment and grief,
Sometimes it lets you fall in love, and then it lets the giddy feeling only fall to abhorrence,
Sometimes it sways you to friendship and belief that you know someone, before that too turns its back on you as nothing but a lie,
But one thing that I have learnt, that life will never be able to take away from me,
Is perseverance, which is a word, that no matter how many times it is broken, it will never leave.
It helps you to fight the devils in life, so you can find the angels,
To knock the doubters away so you can find the believers,
It helps to make sure that every boulder that it hits, it will find a way around, so that the end of the path becomes ever closer,
It helps to shake off the negativity so you only feel the positives,
It will help you gain the knowledge and wisdom that life doesn't always go to plan,
To help you find the true feelings, that you realise is all that matters in life: happiness and love,
It helps to drain all the pain away, so nothing is left but contentment,
And with all this courage, you realise that you find your true pleasure with life,
So that even that, will never bring you down.

Francesca Ottley (13)

OLYMPICS

Vermillion red, electric blue, savannah green, canary yellow and jet black circles flutter in the bright sky
People everywhere trained for this special day, some would go the distance, others would not stay
Competitors all want to go for gold, the rich, the poor and even the old.
Running, jumping, throwing, racing all competing,
Everyone tries their best, however only the chosen few will contest,
Only one can cross the finish line
The winners walk steadily with pride and joy,
 Receiving their reward and reach for the sky
The fans shout and cheer, it is a lovely sound, national music starts
The crowd begins to sing all under the watch of the five coloured rings.
And when the event is over, fans will stop and say,
'I remember you being crowned champion on that special day.'

Priya Badhan (8)

CLEAR AS MORNING

In the doorway to Heaven we're listening to jazz.
It is springtime; as we trail behind death
The blossom is glowing, delicate as porcelain
It can never be as lovely as your smile.
In silence, awkward and overflowing with words
We are seated together, divided by oceans
Of distance, of time, of hopelessness.
I am the secret, the shame in your heart
And this is the fated, unfortunate start
Of futile love. In Death's cold shadow,
The daffodils sing for the afternoon sun.
A cruel tempest is waiting but now
Six years on, your memory drifts into the fire
Until in dreams I see you, clear as morning
Familiar as the days.

Sarah Duncombe

THE MIRROR

You waited all your life for a chance to shine,
Living life each day like everything is fine.
There you are happy, content with your life,
Turning a blind eye to this world's strife,
Ignoring what is right there, thus
You have forgotten about us,
Those who never got the chances,
Chances to up our finances,
Instead we got thrown into the black hole of poverty,
Flood of loans and denied our liberty.

It amazes me how you get richer and we get poorer,
But don't forget, nothing lasts forever.
Don't forget it was *me* that helped you get there,
It was *me* that got you here,
To help you become what you became.
And yet you say I have changed, I am not the same,
What about you?
Are you not the living proof that money is a taboo?
You became corrupted and obsessed,
Obsessed with success,
But one day it will disintegrate into something much less.

You deny me
Forever I'm a part of you, you see,
I am your reflection,
Your intuition
Maybe one day you will remember, remember
What you once were,
So here I am, standing in front of you,
Begging for you to see through,
See through, that thing you wear on your face
That bears nothing but lies and disgrace,
That mask, that façade
So that we can dance to the beautiful ballad,
Of tomorrow's music and rejoice,
That our future is ever so bright because we made the right choice.

Kaozara Oyalowo (16)

WE CAN NEVER BE TOGETHER.

You are up,
I am down,
You are forwards,
I am back,
You are left,
I am right,
We can never be together.

You are round,
I am square,
You are good,
I am bad,
You are an angel,
I am a devil,
We can never be together.

You are east,
I am west,
You are dawn,
I am dusk,
You are the beginning,
I am the end,
We can never be together.

You are on,
I am off,
You are many,
I am none,
You are full,
I am empty,
We can never be together.

You are a cat,
I am a mouse,
You are fire,
I am water,
You are life,
I am death,
We can never be together.

Jessica Kelsey (13)

I REMEMBER . . .

I remember Germany,
The great views of the enormous green hills standing in the distance.
I remember my aunt's house,
On a street with other pretty houses.
I remember the water park,
With many colourful slides.
All of the kids splashing in the water,
Made me just want to jump in.
And the wedding of my aunt,
The beautiful dress, the pile of colourful presents and the three-tier cake.
I remember Germany,
The green, the calm, the place.

Emilija Deveikyte (9)

UNFAIR LAND

Bare are my hands for the skin has darted
Lost in deep sorrow beneath the cracks of slavery.

I work hard and never do I stop
If I do my back will feel the teeth of my master's whip and
I will feel its dreadful slash

I cry every night for my wife and for my children
Who were left behind when me and my wife were towed away
On a boat to float apart from each other for ever

I will one day escape but it will be to the Lord's house
And I will wait for my family there
That's when the pain will stop

But until that day I shall carry on working for the Devil
Being beaten by one of my own kind
And waiting for God's angel to collect me and carry me to safety.

No longer will I eat mouldy bread once a month
But I will feast in God's love in Heaven above.

Kiera Edwards

66

GRANDFATHER

The chair with cigarette burns,
The walls, faintly tinged yellow
From years of nicotine.
The stale smell

And the way the air is heavy,
As if it could choke you.
The ash tray, un-emptied,
Lying on the table.

The box of matches, because
He would never use a lighter.
'Too modern,' he said,
'Too difficult, I'll stick to what I know'.

And what is that?
The chair with the cigarette burns
And the unhealthy air in his lungs.

Katy Gilroy (17)

SCHOOL

At first, I thought things would never be:
Stuck in eternal darkness;
Nothing to do,
Nothing to see,
Not moving on . . .
. . . But what's that?
A light, a light I see!
I've broken from my bonds,
Broken from my cage:
I'm free - as free as a bird in the wind!
I'm going further than I have ever gone before;
The big fish in the small pond.
Suddenly, I feel like a pigeon hunted by a peregrine falcon -
The little fish in the big pond
The older years are ravens and I, a budgie - like my fellow classmates
What will happen?
Will I get out?
Only time will tell . . .

Matthew Chislett (12)

SCHOOL

School is a zoo,
packed full of all sorts of different creatures and beasts
from around the globe, chattering in their many tongues.
As the zoo comes alive,
the playground rapidly becomes full
of screeching screaming monkeys,
gross gargantuan gorillas,
bright beautiful birds,
and the solitary, silent hermit crabs that always get on everyone's nerves.
They roam about their ever-familiar enclosure
until the classes begin,
and, summoned by their persistent keepers,
the animals trudge solemnly and reluctantly back into their cages.
And then all is silent,
apart from the subtle scritchy-scratchy clawed sound of pencils,
the monotonous ramblings of the owls in charge,
and the occasional yell from a particularly rowdy gorilla or a caw of laughter or song from a shrill bird.
At 1 o'clock, the animals excitedly fly out of the door, making a stampede towards the canteen, because it's feeding time.
The carnivores rip apart their burgers, the vegetarians daintily peck at their morsels, and the thin stick insects swarm around the salad bar.
Late in the afternoon, when the last classes have finished,
the animals rush out to attack the visitors.
When everyone leaves, the zoo suddenly, mysteriously closes for the rest of the day due to lack of animals.
And, as quickly as it had become vastly populated only a few hours ago,
it is silent once again.

Edward Sweet (15)

BEING A KID!

Someone asked me a question today which is totally wild,
It was, would you rather be a grown up or a child?

I thought for a second or maybe two,
If I was a grown up oh, what would I do?

I mean there's only cooking and cleaning stuff,
Not like things that'll make me huff and puff

Then I asked my parents what else they have to handle,
Suddenly I was shocked and lit up like a candle

When I found out that they had to go to work,
I would agree I went extremely berserk

I don't want to work in an office wearing a grey suit,
I want to be work free - let the train go *toot, toot!*

I was really surprised about what grownups did,
My decisions not decided yet . . .

I'm just happy being a kid!

Jay Kumra (10)

THOUGHTS OVER THE WEEKEND

Zero is the superhero
First is the nurse
Second is the best
Third is the one with the sparkly dress
Fourth the tidy bedroom
Fifth the poodle princess
Sixth the six-headed monster
Seventh the fairy procession
Eighth the eight-armed alien
Ninth a 99!
Tenth the whole word and everything that rhymes!

Xenia Bahanovich (7)

I WILL ALWAYS MISS YOU

It broke my heart when I knew I'd lost you,
but then I thought to myself
You're not gone, you're inside all of us.
knowing that you're gone I wish I could have done something,
something to stop you from passing on
and leaving my lonely side.
I will always remember your laugh
and your perfect, delightful, sweet personality.
I loved the way you would always smile
no matter what the weather.
If I could spend one more day with you
I would go on a bike ride a thousand times over,
we would talk while we looked across the open river.
These may be things we have done before
but to do them would be amazing.
The fact that you're not standing with me
makes me feel so vulnerable.
I want to be in your arms again.
I don't want to feel your sprit around me anymore.
I want to be reunited with you
but I can't ever see you again.
There are three things I am sure about.
I will always miss you.
I will never forget you.
I will always love you.

Bethany Ann Oxford (13)

A FINAL POEM

To my dearest darling nan,
Up in Heaven, high above,
I know today you're still with us all,
And sending lots of love.

Today, we all remember you,
And bid you one last goodbye,
Celebrate the life you had,
And maybe have a cry.

You'll never be forgotten Nan,
I'll just close my eyes and see,
Your smiling face and feel your love,
And you'll be close to me.

So dear Nan, up above,
Although you are no longer here,
In my heart is where I'll keep you,
Forever, you'll be near.

I see you at the Pearly Gates,
With your little cup of tea,
Please remember that I love you,
As much as you loved me.

You had a very long life,
So many have much less,
There is no doubt, I want to shout,
You really were the best.

Rachel Curtis (13)

THE CURSE OF IMMORTALITY

I walk through the desolate road,
Under the starry midnight sky,
I carry around a heavy load,
Not only my whole life's necessities and memories,
But the heavy load of longing and regret,
I am alone, so lonely, why?
Then I remember my big mistake,
The unlucky turn of fate,
My wish one day thinking,
How wonderful to be immortal
To then turn true, it did,
Then to know, the reality of this,
If only I knew, if only to turn back the hands of time,
Too late, I remind myself, too too late
The world ageing ever more,
Whilst the same, I stay,
Solemnly looking on, in dismay
At the park, I once used to play,
In the playground with my friends,
My father looking over me,
My mother, filled with eyes of love,
My brother and sister, by my side,
I took them all for granted,
Never even said 'thank you,'
For just being there by my side
Watching everyone around you fade away
Isn't right, but my mistake,
The only up, death I do not fear,
But it hurts ever more without it,
Waiting for a miracle to appear,
I see too much, know too much,
Yet with too little experience, or too much,
Things I couldn't imagine,
The homeless and hungry echo pain through their begging hands,
The pungent stench of poverty reeks through the poor,
Only a handful of rice they long,
But cannot have,
Into the frosty windows of a rich merchant I did look,
To see the cook cast away buckets of food
To myself I think, the unfair inequality of life,
I hear nature's cry every day,
Pollution grows by the second,
Bitter litter scattered across the pavements,

Graffiti sprayed over walls and windows
Careless, thoughtless people don't realise the harm they do,
To the world,
As the years go by,
I take the tolls of their consequences,
Of mistreatment to the world
Slowly watching the world fade away, before my eyes
Why, oh why, must I bear this curse?

Thesha Thavaraja (13)

THE GREAT PLAGUE

It was a tragic day in 1664,
When the plague affected few rich, but mainly poor.
A sea of dead bodies,
And even a few dollies.
No clue of what caused the plague,
But now the cause is no longer vague.

Confused children strolling around streets,
Wondering when they and their mother shall meet.
A mother has a sigh of grief,
As she holds her dead baby as their time was very brief.
Cries of frustration as they sit on a log
As they cry, 'Why did this happen God?'

Families and children in so much pain,
How can rich people be so vain?
Destitute children running around,
Making little cries or possibly no sound.

Decomposing bodies lying here and there,
Giving me a little scare.
No child or adult will get better with ease,
So plague . . . go away please!

Vareesha Nasib (11)

SEASONS ARE GREAT

Seasons are great,
There are 4, half of 8,
They're all so different,
In so many ways,

Let's start with winter,
It's snowy and full of white clouds,
It's when the wind whistles so very loud,
You have snowball fights and you make snowmen,
You drink hot chocolate when it turns 10,
So now we are done with winter, what a wonderful season,
Why it's so fun? There is no reason.

Let's move onto autumn,
When all the leaves fall,
Trees grow back up, becoming very tall,
Autumn is so great; you can make piles of leaves,
You go to the back of the yard,
You run at full speed,
You jump in the pile,
You say with a great smile, 'Oh how much fun I have had on this great day,'
So another season gone,
Autumn is so great, it's when you play in the leaves and get mud on your face.

So what can be next?
Oh beautiful spring,
When the flowers come out, and all the birds sing,
This beautiful month is so colourful,
It's blooming with colour; red, white or blue,
You go to a field, pick your favourite flowers,
And the very next day, you go to Alton towers,
What a beautiful season, oh colourful spring,
It is when you go out and play on the swings.

Summer has come, my favourite time of the year,
Is when animals come out, without any fear,
You go on a water slide,
You go to the park and play football,
That's just the start, you wait and you wait for the ice cream man,
Finally you hear the sound of the ice cream van.

You jump up and down in wonderful joy,
Then you line up and wait for your turn,
As if your mouth has burned,
Finally your turn comes; you quickly get a pound from your mum,
So there you have an ice cream in your warm hand,
You eat it all up before anyone can say ten.

There you are with all seasons,
They are so great, beautiful and fun,
But remember this; there are 4, half of 8,
When they passed a year is completely done.

Sheikh Mohsin Abbas (12)

FINISHING LINE

I'm running.
Super-fast.
Out of breath.
The time has passed.
Doing a marathon for Sport Relief.
I have used so much belief
In saving others' lives.
Being there for little fives.
It's there.
Red and white.
Shining there so bold and bright.
Five more minutes – that's all.
All you need to do is crawl.
Slowly in front of the others.
Think of your lively brothers,
John and Chris – so nice.
And your mother with the rice.
30 seconds to go.
Keep on moving – doesn't matter if you're slow.
I'm running.
Super-fast.
Out of breath.
The time has passed.
I feel the wind go down my spine, as I reach the finishing line.

Daisy Williamson (8)

THE DREADFUL DAYS GONE BY

Gunshots, screams and gurgled cries,
Water seeping from the eyes.
To and fro we wonder on,
The battlefield calling us anon.
We the young proud soldiers march,
Passing through France's great arch
Toward the glory of the fight,
To save our nation from a frightful heartless night.

Tears stream from a mothers' eye,
As she bids her first fair son goodbye.
A wrenching scar upon her heart,
Not knowing how long they'll be apart.
Fathers kiss their babes adieu
As a greater life is born anew.

The glory of war still remains unseen . . .

Bullets like a rolling thunderstorm,
Penetrates our regimented form.
Friend and foe drop like flies,
Like everything in this damned land, dies.
Fire spews from a serpent's tongue,
And ignites another man so young.
Blood rains down on the sand,
Like a crimson shadow on the land.
Lost are hopes of glory and fame,
And the only wish is to be home again.

So come now infants, don't delay,
'Your country needs you,' is all they say.
Dreams of war will fill your night,
I only wish I'd never seen this sight.

These are the dreadful days gone by,
What they had said was all a lie.

Morgan Winlock (17)

THE SHADOW

I awake one night,
But I can't see a thing,
Then all of a sudden,
The doorbell rings.

I creep down the stairs,
I look at the time,
It's midnight,
The perfect hour for a crime.

I don't mean crime,
Of burglars and thieves,
I hear a rustle,
In the trees.

I mean the crimes,
Of the shadow at night,
It walks down streets,
Stealing light.

Light means hope,
Love and happiness,
The Shadow means despair,
Hatred and anxiousness.

Trembling fingers,
I open the door,
Not knowing what,
Will stand before.

Blood on his fingers,
A bruise on his knees,
'Can I have,
A plaster please?'

Zoë Martin (12)

SECONDARY SCHOOL

The big fish in the first pond,
But small in the second.
The circle of life goes round,
To this circle we are bound.

Secondary school is very new,
People are nervous, but only a few.
From S1 to S6,
We try to learn life's tricks.

We will try to go far,
It will be the petrol of life's car.
Secondary school will continue to be hard,
It will play a lot of new cards.

In a few years we will see,
What we want to be.
And soon we'll be hurled,
Into the future of the world.

Keshav Mahendra (13)

HER

I saw her sitting staring at me,
Her look was intensely watching, something missing.
Her eyes were buzzing like a bee,
Looking for it, back, forth, left and right.

She sat with an indescribable look.
Some black leather placed on her knees,
It was old-styled, a book.
The intense, concentrated look made me shake.

Ripples went down my spine,
I wasn't who she wanted.
The blood on the carpet like the stain of wine,
That's when I suddenly realised.

The boy on the wall, the one gone,
Once alive, young and free,
He was the one she was looking for, for so long.
She wanted the boy, I'll never be.

The boy she lost long ago,
The one who died,
Her son, the one who had to go.
The replacement, me, was not wanted here.

Caitlin Pittkin (12)

MONDAY MORNINGS

Every morning I wake with the radio on
Playing some hidden meaning song
So with a yawn
And my dismay
No time to play
Start the school day

Brush my teeth, go down the stairs
Seeing grumpy gnarls and stares
My eyes like daggers
As my little brother swaggers
Laughing because it's his day off
I walk out of the lane
Back aching with pain
Schoolbag books that contain
I get more sleep in school than the night before
Because of the constant annoying snore

As the bell rings, I pack my things
I go to bed, with a sore head
My eyes are red, from all the pages I've read
I fall asleep and wake again to my dread.

Stephen Bell (14)

ODE TO WINTER

This glorious winter,
Capture the moment.
The sharp wind
Slapping across your face.
Ice-cold hands.
Fingertips freezing.
The silky snow
Twirling and prancing.
Snowflakes delicately dancing
Like a breath of wind.
Cherish your memorable time with nature.
The frosts glitter, sparkle
Around the
Snowy blanket.
Oh, joyful times.
Where's the beaming sun?
And the golden glow?
It has vanished.
It has perished.
Until the very next year.

Ferial Bezchi (11)

I'M A GIRL

I'm a girl, just a girl
I like to sing, I like to twirl,
Dressed in pink and feeling pretty,
Hello Barbie, Hello Kitty

I'm a girl, I'm a girl
Watch my attitude unfurl
I'm starting to think . . .
That I don't need . . .
To be all swishy haired and golden
Like a mini Amanda Holden.
Don't want to be another Cheryl Cole
With rinky, slinky hips
Shiny hair and pouty lips
Don't need to cover up my face
With stuff that is so fake.
Crushed strawberry juice will stain my lips,
Wind-whipped cheeks blush in the sun
A manicure of mud
And rain clouds dropping sparkling diamonds into my hair.

I'm a girl, yeah, a girl
And I can shout, laugh, scream, giggle
Or my lip can curl, if I want
I can run barefoot through the dewy grass and not cry if I step on a thistle
I can roller skate at the speed of light
Last week I climbed Mount Everest (in my mind)
Maybe one day I will!
Who knows what I will find to do?
Who gets to choose,
Whether I stay or go, win or lose?
It's up to me,
Not my parents, my teachers, my friends
Not even you.
Cos I'm a climber of trees,
Scraper of knees,
Word weaver,
Dog-walking diva,
Gonna grow taller than my brother,
Be a person like no other,
Dreaming of glory
This is my story.

I'm Grace,
This is my face,
This is me.

Grace Maltman (9)

NO THRONES

The coolness, it turns to lava,
The softness, it turns to stone.
The princess gets to her feet,
She doesn't want the throne.

The lightness, it turns to charcoal,
The summer, it turns to snow.
The queen looks for her daughter,
The princess she doesn't know.

The steeple, it turns to sawdust,
The cathedral, it turns to straw.
The king looks for the prince,
For the son he never saw.

The windows, they turn to paper,
The sashes, they turn to glue.
The prince turns to the princess,
The sister he never knew.

The throne, it turns to wood,
No golden guilt, no stones.
The family, they turn to dolls,
No feeling, no love . . . no thrones.

Emily Rose Vincent (14)

WING OF FIRE

I was flying over the village
On Bonfire night
When a little girl screamed
And gave me a fright!

My wing caught on fire,
It seared with pain,
Hurling towards the village,
In a ball of flame.
I fell to the earth,
And bashed on the ground,
Then all the villagers
Gathered around.

A man came up
And looked at them all,
And said, let's finish him off
Once and for all.

Everyone cheered at what he said,
At that minute, I knew I was dead.
Then an old lady in her hand a potion,
Very surprisingly slipped through the commotion.

And then I was off
Quick as a wink,
And now wherever I go
I have to think.

I know to stay away from Bonfire night,
The village, the men,
And that girl I gave a fright.

Smruti Gupte (11)

SOMEDAY

Can you still see me? Are you still here?
How do I know that you are near?

It is cruel that you left me, here all alone,
I can't talk to you, listen to you moan.

Despite all that moaning, I still love you, you know,
I never expected you to just go,

Do you still love me? Do you know I care?
Do you know each night for you I say a prayer?

I want you here with me, to sing to me again,
For when you're not with me it isn't the same.

I need to be with you, I love you so much
I need the comfort of your soft touch.

What is it like there, up in the sky?
I want to join you but I can't, why?

I hope you still watch me, in all that I do,
I want you to be proud of me like you used to.

If I am patient, the time will arrive,
For us to be re-united and then we will thrive,

But for now I will live, live life to the full,
Despite my emotions which rage like a bull.

Please wait for me, don't go away,
I will come to join you, someday.

Josie Foster (13)

NEAREST AND DEAREST

Across and across we go
The highs and lows we go through
All together but some things in life do not show
It is what the above chose
We can't change what happened
But we can look back at those sweet times
That singing, chatting and rhymes

When we run
When we hide
We don't know how they feel about us now
When we have fun
When we lied
They will always forgive and give the occasional eyebrow

They go through so much pain
The load of amount is completely insane
But they know we're here
And we will never let them cry or let out a single tear

Times are tough
So you learn to look after
But sometimes you have enough
Gradually you'll feel proud which ends up in laughter

Unbreen Shabnum Aziz (13)

ODE TO SUMMER

This season is colourful,
Colourful as rainbows,
As tasty like mangoes.
The sun
Shines down
Its rays sparkle
In the summer air
So still,
Not a breath of wind.
Butterflies
And bumblebees
Charmed to flowers
Flutter
And buzz
In summer.
Ladybirds perching
On emerald green leaves
Of summer trees.
This
Moment
Under blue skies
Grab it,
Don't let it slip away!
Stay trapped,
In the moment
Forever
Because it sparkles
Glimmers
Shimmers
Like a star,
Under the sapphire night sky!

Siobhan Willers (10)

MY IMAGINATION

My imagination is orange,
Cool yet exciting
It is fizzy and bubbly,
Like a can of Fanta.

My imagination is a puppy,
Playful and fun
It is like candyfloss,
Bursting with flavour.

My imagination is a money tree,
Rich with cash
It is a flowing dress,
Going everywhere.

My imagination is a tennis ball
Bouncing all around
It is a bed
Sleepy and tired.

My imagination
Bursting with success.

Mohini Karhadkar (10)

MY IMAGINATION

My imagination is a fluffy cloud
It floats around collecting little droplets
It is silk
A soft touch
It is like a natural spring
Bubbling up.

My imagination is a Sky Hawk
Soaring through the clouds
If it were a colour,
It would be yellow
Joyful and cheerful
It is a flute
Calm and relaxing

My imagination is a puppy
Loyal and playful
It is chocolate
Tasty and sweet
Mmmm . . . yum

My imagination is . . .
What should I write?

Meenal Alagappan (9)

BULLY 4 U

Hair combed back, collar neat,
Everything perfect; from head down to feet.
Surrounded by people older and bigger,
Childish and small, I feel like Tigger.
All they do is talk (what a drag!),
To be honest I'd rather play tag.
An older boy approached me,
Giant and tall from what I could see.
He grabbed my bag and I told him to give it back,
But he just laughed and emptied my pack.
Took my belongings, purse and phone,
Threw me to the ground and left me alone.
Nobody around me really cares,
I just sat there crying on the stairs.
But I've changed now, a bully at name,
I guess it was time to raise my game.
People may call me sick and sad,
But that was because my past was bad.
I steal money and bags, phones too,
But you have to get them . . . before they get you.

Lauren Taylor (11)

ODE TO WINTER

This season
Is as cold
As an iceberg
And as white
As the whites of your eyes.

Arrives like a gift
From the skies
Is a parcel of snow.

Ice-cold
Hearts,
Freezing
Fingertips.

The golden glow
Of summer
Has waved
Goodbye

Cherish
The cold
And the snow
While it lasts.

Subana Khalid (10)

A PEACEFUL OCEAN OF TROUBLE

Not a lake,
Not a creek
Not a pond,
But the deep

The fish I meet are ever so rare,
Piranhas,
Anglerfish,
Everything is there!

Coral orange,
Marine shades of blue,
Bottomless sandy bed,
Some algae too

Mermaids hidden in their mystical world,
Treasure chests overflowing with diamonds and pearls

Then all darkens,
Unpleasant to meet,
Comes a huge grey shark,
Desperate to eat!

Crashes,
Bashes,
Water lashes
The waves' soothing roar,
I've heard it before,
Along the lapping rhythmic seashore

Tears of timorous ripples,
They hide as I swim by,
I gasp, a salty mouthful of water,
From this endless aqua supply

A dangerous place,
The deep sea,
If you're daring to explore,
Then you're just like me!

Caitlin Amy Watts (12)

SOMEDAY

The value of life is decreased every day,
Some of us think there's no point in living if a hurdle comes our way.
We always give up and a second time we never try,
But life has to go on, over spilt milk we shouldn't cry.

We don't realise how lucky we are,
There are people out there who are in worse situations by far.
Normally we take the shorter path and hardly go the full mile,
But when you take it on you'll see it was actually worth your while.

Look at others as our inspirations,
Using them as our guides we shall strengthen our determination.
As time goes on, life's struggles we shall face,
But we have to be positive then we can ace.

Life can be complex and we all have our dreams,
Something we wish for, something supreme.
Those things that we want we can all achieve,
So long as we keep going, as long as we believe.

The melancholic things that are remembered we should erase,
On memory lane contentment should be our base.
The negative energy and emotions we should overwrite,
It is hope and faith that we should incite.

Opportunities come and go but sometimes we don't recognise,
Our chance and possibility are right in front of our eyes.
Every time we fail we like to moan and lament,
Instead of wasting time like that we should try again to the furthest extent.

Life flies by and we take it all for granted,
When things go wrong you can't blame anyone else as it was the seed you planted.
It doesn't matter if things go wrong as you can always make them right,
Where there's a will there's a way and with happiness you can always reunite.

In this world filled with changes every single day,
The sky should be the limit and we should not be lead astray.
To our younger we should try and be their role models and portray,
Our dreams are at the end of the rainbow and we will get there someday.

Aliya Manji (14)

THANK YOU

To you I am thankful
Thankful for the life you have given me
For this opportunity to live
I will not disappoint you, you will see

You are handed the bundle
And wrapped within the snow-white bundle is me
You look at me with such love and joy in your eyes
Oblivious to what awaits . . .

A year has passed
I have now discovered the art of walking
This new skill allows me to create mischief,
On the sight of food I run and hide

At the age of three,
I attend nursery
You leave me there, with strangers
A new place with lots of toys, but these don't comfort me
I cry, with fear in my eyes, I cling to you, but
They don't let you stay
In silence I anticipate your return

I am now five,
We are in an aeroplane - it's chaotic and noisy
With your comfort I survive the journey
We arrive at our destination
This is your motherland, but to me it is foreign
I hide behind your back as you greet your relations

At eleven I start secondary school
My mood changes
It's all about make-up and friendship groups now
What's in and what's out
Keeping up with the latest fashions dominates my mind

Over the coming years, I bring tears to your eyes
My harsh words hurt you
You see my character change and develop
Until, finally I reach a mature young adult

I look after you as you fight for your health
I regret all the times I've argued with you
Days on end I'm separated from you
Thanks to God you return home
And slowly I have the old you back
I am now 17,

I accept my newly discovered freedom
With the hope that I can fulfil both our dreams
I learn to laugh and relax

Soon I will leave, but I promise I will return
I won't go too far,
And even if I do, I will be close to your heart
So I say thanks
Thanks for spending those sleepless nights nursing me
I am grateful for all you have done
I love you, Mum.

Mariam Khan (17)

BROKEN

Her eyes burn like fire,

Her heart's made of ice.

Her every action, a gamble,

A roll of the dice.

Inside her soul is shattering, breaking,

Endless pain behind the smile she is faking.

Her strength is gone,

Her willpower weakening,

Her grief apparent in every word she is speaking.

Behind the mask you can see the starkness,

Her once-bright soul giving in to the darkness.

Madeleine Thomson (14)

THE OLD OAK'S SMILE

The gnarled old oak tree gave,
What to him,
Was a smile,
Flaked leaves on his moustache sagged a little less,
And his icy Afro stood on end.

Winds hurled debris,
Embittered air,
Rain,
And a spiky chill.

Logs rolled down the bleak hillside,
Were compressed and packaged,
And sold.

The gnarled old oak tree was sharpened,
And pressed against his rigid skin,
Etched onto the gnarled old oak tree,
Was himself.

Olivia Rix (11)

THE JOURNEY OF A PENNY

The one pence penny starts its journey in a purse full of many
It's traded far but rarely used
As it is a coin not everyone will choose
But what they don't realise is that it can go far
Grouped together you can buy a chocolate bar

The one pence penny can be found in the deep
Or even rolling along an avenue or street
If it falls in a gutter
It will join one and another
If you find a penny it brings you luck
So always remember to pick it up

But when you scuffle through your bag
And all you can find is your name tag
Remember how your special penny was found
All you have to do is look to the ground
If it's not there and you have searched plenty
It has continued its journey across purses of many.

Kazim Manji (11)

96

ENGLISH LESSONS

I want to know
Why I don't like English
Lessons, that is
I love reading, writing, imagining,
So why is it
This subject eludes me?
I don't understand
Why we need to know
Why the writer put
That the sky was blue
Who cares?
It's blue
That's all that matters
Getting lost
In a world that a genius
Created
What's the point
In writing reams and reams
Of things that
I bet the writer
Didn't think about?
I don't know if
What they put
Has a hidden meaning
And if it's good
I don't want to
Look too deeply
I want
To let it all
Just wash over me
I've been told not
To be so childish
Churlish and silly
But I really am
Trying to be mature
I just don't understand
Why literature
Is ruined
In English lessons.

Freya Clarke (13)

WRAITH

I didn't know what was happening.
You all surrounded me.
You all looked down.
You touched my hand.

Unaware of why, you wanted the answer.
What happened?

You all walked away.
They shut me in, they locked the door.
I was trapped.
They closed the case.
They pushed me away.
I need to know why.
Everyone should know.
I'll be like this forever.
There is nothing I can do.
I'll seek for the answer.
But there is no guarantee. I've been forgotten now.
Years have passed by.
No one can see me or feel me.
I'm stuck like this.
I need to find out who did this.
I've hit a brick wall.
I'm left without an answer.

Paige Morgan Medway (13)

PARADISE

Something straight ahead of me is glistening in the sunlight like precious jewels dazzling in the moonlight.
I take a small step and something warm and soft strokes the bottom of my feet.
Paradise.
The golden sand around me runs through my fingers letting the swift breeze land it with a be-witching whisper.
The alluring sand beneath me blows with such elegance it is unreal.
Paradise.
Noting every grain of sand I walk, mesmerised by my surroundings towards the clear turquoise sea.
Hesitating, I gradually let my foot slip into the crystal ocean.
Paradise.
My whole body slides in as the natural beauty lures me into the depths of the water.
 I cannot remember the world from where I came, with its litter and crowds in contrast to such a clear and majestic environment.
Paradise.
Leaving the ocean behind I find something else to admire knowing there will be another fascina-tion ahead.
Soon, I sit and gaze up at the dancing palm trees swaying in time with the breeze.
Paradise.
I watch, as coconuts fall landing with a gentle thump as they collide with the sand on the ground.
Desperately wanting to taste some I knock the coconut onto the firm trunk of the tree that it grew on.
To my surprise it opens. I take a bite and the coconut tastes more glorious than the finest mango.
Paradise.
I feel like I am in heaven now.
I lie on the delicate sand looking up where the sun shines like precious amber.
It has a welcoming touch of warmth and makes me feel as if I belong.
Paradise.
The brightness of the sun lights the island like a lamp.
My dream of visiting paradise has come true!

Safia Safdar (9)

THE UNKNOWN, THE LOST, THE WANTED

As I sang my heart out
I heard a shout
The stage was unknown
As I was suddenly alone
For I was lost
I was no longer star crossed
As I started to pack
I was ambushed in an attack
For I lost all that was wanted
Then I was cheated
For I am the unknown
For I am the wanted
For I am lost
In the world below
As my heart was pierced
I lost all thought
As my skin was slit
I take the knife
And throw it as far as possible
For I want to survive
In love
I'm wanted
I'm lost
I'm the unknown
That takes your life
When least expected
I am
The unknown
The lost
The wanted
For my life to survive
I have to be alive
For my lost love are you
Here I can say
Today
I survive
For I am
The unknown
The lost and the wanted
You believe in me
I believe in you
I am in denial
Of my true love

Surviving till the end
As this is me
Hidden away in the Caspian Sea
As I disappear
You think
And remember how I am
The unknown
The lost
The wanted.

Matthew Lonsdale (15)

SERENITY OF SPRING

The delicate blushing of the cherry blossoms kiss the
land below - tenderly, sweetly, like the fragrance of
a graceful rose.

Petals float like tranquil feathers, producing an
entrancing glow - dancing, romancing, casting away
all depressing woes.

Ebony as night, shadows pirouette and begin their
eternal flight,
Leaving only the rich landscape of gentle fuchsia and
royal azure in its luminous sight.

Lush grass flutters like a butterfly's majestic wings,
The rhythm, the tempo, it's like the chartreuse sings,
An ethereal melody of sweet amity and gentle felicity,
Purifying all malicious intent with angelic serenity.

This is the blissful essence of the season *spring*.

Klaudia Rafinska (12)

I GIVE . . .

I give to you deep, salty seas,
But you give me oil spills in return.
I give to you fishes of all kinds,
But you give me piles of plastic.

I give you beautiful nature and trees,
But you give me forest fires in return.
I give you flowers and bees,
But you suffocate them with smog.

I give you fresh air to breathe in,
But you choke me with gas and smoke.
I give you luscious land to live in,
But you use me as a dump for sharp bottles and glass.

I have given you too many chances,
One after the other.
Just stop, and think
What can I do to help?

Olivia Gikas (11)

THE STEEL HUNTING KNIFE

The steel left no stain,
It pushed deep through the skin,
And withdrew clean and clear,
No recognition of the pain it caused.
The victim gasped for air,
The knife was clutched in the huntsman's hand.
His quest was complete,
 He started to search for another,
Endless torment approached everything he met.
The huntsman stepped away,
The victim called after him,
She begged him to be set free,
He didn't hear the shrieks,
He didn't hear the cries,
He didn't hear the pain inside.
He lived with no regrets,
But when time turned
The huntsman became the hunted.
The steel left no stain,
It pushed deep through the skin,
And withdrew clean and clear.

Jazmyn Barlow (16)

WALKABOUT

A new day dawns,
And out in the Australian outback
Siblings are thirsty,
Hidden in a crack.

>   Out in the outback,
>   You know not where nor when.
>   One black, two white.
>   One dies, two survive.

The plane has crashed,
And the flames shoot towards the heavens,
Where all must surely be.
All but two.

>   Out in the outback,
>   You know not where nor when.
>   One black, two white.
>   One dies, two survive.

The bush boy,
On his walkabout, meets the children.
To survive six months, alone.
To prove men.

>   Out in the outback,
>   You know not where nor when.
>   One black, two white.
>   One dies, two survive.

They meet, black and white,
A species the other has not seen.
Three different cultures,
But the same within.

>   Out in the outback,
>   You know not where nor when.
>   One black, two white.
>   One dies, two survive.

The girl sees death.
The tears from her, cried by her brother.
The bush boy dies.
Their ideals change.

Out in the outback,
You know not where nor when.
One black, two white.
One dies, two survive.

The journey remains,
To find civilisation: with a loss.
Friends and helpers.
A big, big loss.

Out in the outback,
You know not where nor when.
One black, two white.
One dies, two survive.

Enjoy life,
It does not last forever,
It matters not of the shell,
But of what is within.

Out in the outback,
The loss you feel is great.
Friends in the unnatural.
One dies, two survive.

Celia Stoddart (13)

JUST AS WE USED TO

I would sit upon your lap and cuddle in tight,
You would tell a bedtime story and tuck me in at night.
I wish things were still the same and nothing had changed in you
I still hope we can do things just as we used to.

There are no more hugs and kisses just before I go
I might be growing up but I hope that you still know
I love you with all my heart
And nothing could tear us apart.
I wish I wasn't older and I didn't have to leave you
I really wish we could stay the same and be just like we used to.

Caitlin Griffiths (11)

NO MORE GAMES

There are no more games the world can play,
There are no more lives, no second day.
If you think like a child, you'll understand,
We cannot trust who's in command.

From the tiny towns, to the mighty states,
There are people affected by your mistakes.
From your misdeeds, your doings of wrong,
People are ignored, yet they do belong.

What are you doing with all of this?
You're millionaires! You're living in bliss!
But do you care? Do you even know?
The world has lost its warming glow.

Can you do all these things you say you can do?
You're tearing down old and building things new.
You're destroying the Earth, in all of its glory,
The trauma on the news is someone's life-story.

What kick-started all this fuss?
Was it banks, or one of us?
All are greedy for money and power,
The natural world, we shall devour.

And yes, I know I'm just a child,
I like to play, run round, be wild!
But the changes you make affect my life,
I grow up in a world of worry and strife.

So now I give you one last chance,
To give more to the world, than a simple glance,
You can change our future with one single word:
Say yes to the people, so we can be heard.

Hannah Ost (12)

106

THE MOUSE

He races along the lumpy ground,
Avoiding the teeth
Of the menacing hound;
Running, running
For all he was worth;
Dashing along
The grassy turf.

As fast as a hawk,
He ran and ran;
There!
There was his nest;
And finally he knew,
That at last
He could rest.

Tom Griffiths (12)

BLOOD AND TEARDROPS . . .

Tears fall from the eyes of friendship,
And darkness reigns,
The wind blows my heart away,
And sends me broken pains,
Blood and teardrops somewhere lay,
Deeper, deeper in my heart,
I thought she'd be there for me,
That we'd never part,
My eyes start pounding,
Ready to cry,
But the love between us,
It will never die,
You'll always be there for me,
You'll be there 'til the end,

'Cause you're my best friend . . .

Emily Blake (12)

A SOLDIER IN MIND

I have a little story that I'd adore to tell,
I mean, it's something quite spectacular,
Then I suppose I might as well,
There was once this little boy,
Whose name I must conceal,
Now he means the world to me,
That's the one thing that I'll reveal,
He used to be a solider see,
Who fought in many wars,
He tried his best I swear,
And made his country proud, I promise,
That's another thing I'll declare,
He used to wake up at the crack of dawn,
Never really complained,
He'd just smile and yawn,
He would protect his country with such a modest tone,
Risk his life, yet never save his own,
You see now I look at him,
And see a true hero smiling back,
With every limb in place,
This hero, this solider,
I can never displace,
I used to often sit in his chair,
Mocking his actions.
As he would slyly stare,
This man was a hero, a brave solider I swear,

Even till this day,
That gleam's still there.
He's all grown up now,
Grey and old you see,
This hero, this solider, this man
I call him my dad-dy
I have a little story that I'd adore to tell,
I mean, it's something quite spectacular to me,
Then I suppose I might as well.

Kadife Toci (14)

EMOTIONS

Happiness is weekends, no school,
Sadness is lessons, so dull,
Disappointment is work too tough,
Anxiety is, 'Have I done enough?'
Worried is taking home a school report,
Stress is holidays too short,
Fun is creative, that you never forget,
Boring is work with little effect,
Tiredness is lessons in the sun,
Relaxation in school never does come,
Enjoyable is always the best time,
Angry sometime feels like a crime.

School is school; it's either good or bad,
Though I know when I leave I'll be sad!

Ayesha Hassan (13)

WATCHFUL EYES

As the darkness folds its arms
around the raging sun
and the stars come out to shine
and to blink at me,
I think of the moon and how
the night protects me
Now I rest as the stars keep their
watchful eyes twinkling
Tomorrow there will be sunlight
to chase away the darkness;
now the stars close their eyes
until dusk comes again.

Clair Louisa Bellarby (12)

HEAR MY STORY OUT

I was seven years of age
And on my seventh year I learnt
To hold one's family close to heart
And the death of one had burnt
My beliefs of an idealistic world
And the innocence of youth
The dreams of flying to candyfloss clouds
And sharing such wonders with you

Seven years have passed now
Since my seventh year of age
And still my child-like, care-free mind
Refuses to engage
Truth is I grew up cold
And bitter to the core
No matter what life offered me
I was constantly searching for more

Now hold the pity, hold the moans
Please hear my story out
I'm not a 'hate on life teenager,'
Who drinks and fights and shouts
You left me and vanished hope
When I was seven years of age
They told me, 'It's the story of life!
Just move on, just turn the page,'

But how was I to carry on?
Confused
Disappointed
Alone
My little cousin had died so young
Without a whisper of 'hello,'
My God had failed to answer prayers
All adults had tried their best
But doctors, surgeons, even priests
Had failed the Devil's test

Unwillingly you went away
And with no sign of guilt he stole
Your fragile body, your innocent mind
And my – now shattered – soul
I hear you ask in desperation,
'How is this not hating on life?'
But to see the light in a situation

One must first understand the strife
When a child of youth, faces death
Say, seven years of age
Their imagination fails, defences go up . . .
Their smiles begin to fade
I tell you this, I know all too well
It is impossible to understand
The pain of losing a relative
If you have not so much as held their hand

You see I'd never met my cousin
Never seen his perfect face
But his death tore all love out of me
And such can never be replaced
So I ask of you to cast your minds
On the 'chavs', the 'thugs', and 'rebels',
Do you think they would behave in such a way?
If they had not witnessed Hell

So my theory here today
And by God I know it's true
Is, that in every single memory
Of every one of you
You've generalized us teenagers
On what the media allows you to see
But what your eyes fail to understand
Is the pain
The hurt
The grief

So all we're asking is for your help
Please help us understand
Why we can't smile
We can't love
We can't hold out a hand
See we cannot come to terms with
Why we are so confused
Why can't others feel the pain we do?
We want others to feel alone, to feel used

So we're searching for someone, anyone
To feel our hurt the same
And when it's clear we have not found it
We set off and search again
But eventually we realise
No one feels the pain we do
So we destroy whatever we have found

And you put it down to an 'act of our youth',
It's stupid, it doesn't help
At best it's really selfish
But what do you expect from a Class A muck-up?
We are just kids
Kids who've been left alone
Abandoned and completely torn apart
We might not have a soul
But what you fail to realise is we've got heart!

So give us the time of day,
Help us and eventually you'll see
We've got dreams
We've got so much love to give
We've got things we want to be!

So no
I'm not a 'hate on life teenager'
Who drinks and fights and shouts
But I could have been
Maybe I was . . .

Until, someone heard my story out.

Nicole-Shola Edwards (14)

LIFE

Wind blows through the air,
So softly there and there.
Birds drift down below,
I was enjoying the breeze,
So very slow.

Slowly, gently, softly too,
The wind blows through me and you,
Love flows through our hearts.
Hopefully it shall last.

Samuel Taylor (12)

DISTRACTIONS

My mum calls me mental,
My dad calls it bad,
I have to stop fiddling,
Or I'll make people mad...

The twiddle of my pencil,
My knuckles when they click,
Irritating habits,
That creates a lunatic . . .

The adrenaline is buzzing,
I'm losing my will,
People are shouting,
Just sit still!

Fingers tapping on the keyboard,
It makes people sick,
Irritating habits,
That creates a lunatic . . .

Dropping lots of objects,
Drives people up the wall,
'Dan put your shoes away!'
'No, I need to make a call . . . '

Making someone crazy,
I know every trick,
Irritating habits,
That creates a lunatic . . .

Distractions are awful,
Horrible and cruel,
You make think I'm insane,
But I'm certainly not a fool . . .

Daniel Brannan (13)

HANSEL AND GRETEL PARODY

One beautiful summer's day,
An evil step-mum was cooking away,
She was a step-mum to Gretel and Hansel,
But she wished their birth was something to cancel.

Then that evening she kicked them out
The dad said, 'Hey just wait about!
Why kick the kids out the door?'
Mum said, 'I hate them forever and more!'

So Gretel and Hansel were trapped in the wood
They honestly didn't know how they could,
Get out of that damp, dark jail,
I'm not kidding, they looked so pale!

Then they found a sweet house,
As fast as a cheetah, they pounced,
Chocolates, toffees, and candy-canes,
Hansel and Gretel thought they were going insane!

Suddenly, an old lady opened the door,
And said, 'Come in and have some more!
Then I'll make us a cup of tea
So then you can spend some time with me!'

'Go in the oven to see if it's hot,
If it is, then grab the pot!'
She called to Hansel, he burnt his shin,
Then the evil lady locked him in!

'Please old lady, let him out!'
'No, my dear!' she began to shout
Then she ran and grabbed a dirk,
'Now, you must get to work!'

The dad and step-mum found the house,
In they crept, silent as a mouse,
They found poor Hansel in a cage,
Then the old lady went into a rage!

The old lady had a breakdown,
They were all laughing, smiling like clowns,
Then the lady grabbed the step-mum,
And said, 'Oh be gone!'

So the kids and the dad went back home,
And to celebrate they had ice cream cones,
They jumped up and down, and cheered,
Finally, they had nothing to fear!

Raina Raval (10)

SNOW

Here it comes,
It fills me with dread,
No, it's not thunder and lightning,
It is snow instead!

Snow that coats the land,
Like icing on top of a cake,
It paints the world white,
And makes everything beautiful in its wake!

And yet more is coming,
Oh what a sight!
Still more is falling,
I fear it will block out the light!

I see no people,
The roads are deserted!
We are trapped in our homes!
The police must be alerted!

I no longer hear the robins,
That so joyfully sang,
It saddens my heart,
I doubt that I will hear them again.

The sun is coming,
According to the news,
It shall melt the snow,
And replace it with slush that shall soak our shoes!

The snow has all melted,
We are free at last,
No longer trapped,
No, that is all in the past.

Hannah Morgan (15)

SECRECY

Silence. Seconds tick by. My fingers
Squeeze the pen, my tips becoming
Inky red blobs as I sit there, waiting.

I sit for a long time, as seconds turn
To minutes, and long forgotten
Chores return to mind. Swimming
Round and round, taunting me.
Mocking me.

I've got it!

My hands start shaking.
I imagine them as withered thin bones,
With long yellowed nails, and then there's me,
Cackling delightedly as my mind starts to flow,
Transferring from my head to crisp, chalky paper.

Transferring my thoughts, feelings.
Everything I was, everything I will and everything I want to be.
Every little quote and line from mismatched nothings.
Every tiny doodle and picture from the depths of my brain.
Every burst of music that brings hope and life.
Every powerful memory that I can't forget,
Happy and sad.

The sadness. The grief. The regret.
Every pitiful moment I wish I could
Change, and every moment I wished
Never existed. All the broken
Sentiments which for the life of me I wished could be
Fixed.

And then there's the brilliance.
The spark of fire on an empty starless night,
Spreading and spreading to destroy the cancerous oblivion
Which obviously only exists in my mind.

The genius that I created-
Well, maybe not genius, but it feels like it to me, and so it shall remain till the
Harsh words of one void spectator destroys it
In a moment of my weakness.

And then it fades.

So I sit there.

116

Silence. Seconds tick by. My fingers
Squeeze the pen, my tips becoming
Inky red blobs as I sit there, waiting.

Lauren Pittkin (15)

PAINTING A PICTURE

Azure sky with flecks of white,
Aimless clouds just floating by,
Rolling hills of deepest green,
To the lightest emerald ever seen.
Fences and hedges splitting the land,
Some rich soil, the rest copper sand,
Dots of white wool scattered on top,
From outlying rocks, heart racing drops.
Flocks of gold flowers make up a field,
Under their petals bugs are concealed,
A ray of sun shines down on the ground,
The wind fills the valley with light breezy sound.
And nestled in the crook of the giant green hill,
A writer sits with his scribbling quill,
He writes of the landscape that is shifting behind,
He's painting a picture that comes from the mind.

Molly Jankowski (12)

NOTHING AND EVERYTHING

Like thousands of unsettled butterflies they float around,
Dodging thought clouds and overcoming any thought of sanity or salvation,
Things that have not been told, things that are never thought drift across my now sleepy state,
The guard has been given up and the foes are attacking the mind.
Glass shatters and the shards reverberate inside my now hollow head,
This continuous loop of breakages perplexes my now wide-awake mind,
And how can the night make subtle thoughts unbearable?
Everything breaks up in a dreamlike state,
Immense worries become thousands of fluttering creatures,
Whereas the smallest inkling of negative thought grows and increases till it breaks,
And the loop of broken thoughts starts again.

Kyle Power (17)

THE GIRL IN THE GLASS

The girl in the glass,
Stares through the shine,
Her eyes, they water,
Frozen in time.

A curse holds her there,
So great is this power,
A tear frozen on her cheek,
As she stands in her tower.

The door is sealed,
With bricks and magic,
Can her life,
Be any more tragic?

Sleep never comes,
Her eyes will not close,
She will stand there forever,
For her, time has frozen.

Lost in the wind,
Are her cries for help,
No one will come,
And her heart will melt,
The village is empty,
The people have fled,
The statue above them,
Filled them with dread.

There is only one way,
To break the curse,
And that is death,
By far the worst.

She does not age,
As the years fly by,
People come and go,
She does not die.

Years later,
She feels a twitch,
Behind her stands,
That evil old witch.

She casts a spell,
And cackles with glee,
As the girl drops down,
With no one to see.

The witch has departed,
The girl met her death,
So now she sleeps,
Without a breath.

Rea Sachdeva (11)

PEOPLE PLAYING

People playing hopscotch,
In the sun,
All day long,
Having great fun.

People skipping,
every day,
having fun,
in every way.

Playing footy,
with their friends,
Hoping the game,
will never end.

Playing outside,
is good for you,
doing everything,
we want to do.

Sean Webster (7)

119

ASLEEP OR AWAKE!

Sun shining bright as day,
Nothing stands in my way.
Brothers, sisters, Mum and Dad,
These are the people I never had.

Finding shelter is so hard,
For my blanket I use some card.
Why am I filled with such hate?
Why can't this be simple, am I some sort of bait?

Scrounging money may get in my way,
Just another boring day.
My shoes are in such a state,
Another thing that I hate.

I kneel before my god's feet,
It's like He's here like I can feel His heat.
Then there are sudden screams and yelps,
'Help him!' someone cries. 'Go get help!'

There's blood, blood all around,
Everyone's lips are moving but they don't make a sound.
I'm spinning, tumbling, round and round,
Until I finally touch the ground.

Everything is so dark and black,
I turn and get a sharp pain in my back.
Suddenly a bright light, I climb the steps of stone,
A calm voice whispers, I look around, I'm all alone.

Then I start shaking,
Crying, my body's aching.
Then a man appears,
I suddenly can hear.

It's my father, my mother's there too,
My wishes and dreams have finally come true.
So it never happened, it was all just a dream,
So I wasn't dead or hadn't been?

I open my eyes, I'm lying down,
I get up still wearing my frown.
I just hate and hate,
I keep telling myself I'm no one's bait.

I move my cold blanket of card,
I still feel the cold stone digging into my back, hard.
So I'm asleep or awake,
But my body does still ache.

Sun shining, bright as day,
Nothing stands in my way.
Brothers, sisters, Mum and Dad,
These are the people I never had.

Elizabeth Drake (14)

NIGHTMARE

A drop of death
The invasion of fear
Distant screams,
Are all that I hear.

Footsteps creep behind me
But I'm blind in the darkness,
So I can't see.

A howl from a werewolf
A bite from a vampire
These are the things, I don't desire
A lake of blood
The dance of a skeleton
A pile of dead bodies
Argh! I'm done.

Saubhagya Moktan (9)

THE CHILD OF NATURE

Tears well up in my eyes
As my feelings rise to the top.
Why me? Why only me?
They torment me,
They give me nightmares,
They are the dark side.

Cries of mirth and glee are heard,
As they come, closer and closer
And yet no one can see them,
They are invisible,
That is, until the night approaches,
They burst upon their prey,
They feed on their terror.
I strive to cry silently
I know that I must not make a sound,
But alas, my tears are cunning,
They escape from my clumsy fingers
And drop one by one, like priceless black pearls,
Priceless for they give me away.

The world stops,
A ghastly silence falls around me,
I can feel their eyes,
Pools of fire, thirsty for mortal terror,
Looking at me.
I can feel their deathly presence
As their light fingers reach out to touch my soul.
When one of them touches me,
I fall to the ground
My body as heavy as lead, as cold as ice.
They scream, it is shrill and high-pitched,
It makes my ears ring
And then they stop.
It happens so quickly, any mortal eye would fail to catch it,
The first rays of sunlight filter through them,
And they are ripped to shreds.

My heart pumps and thumps in joy,
Birds burst into songs of life
Animals leap and fly over me,
Telling me that it is over
I am alive and changed.
I can count every vein in a leaf,
I can see the world in iridescent colours as I never could before.

122

Happiness runs through me like a young deer
As my world changes.
Each droplet of water is as beautiful as diamonds,
Each blade of grass as precious as stripes of emeralds
And each lake a pure and deep as molten sapphire.
My world has changed yet remains unchanged
My feelings are pure,
I am a child of nature.

Rupali Dabas (13)

I KEEP SANTA IN THE CELLAR

I keep Santa in the cellar
To try and slim him down;
He only eats once a day,
And always with a frown.

I keep Santa in the cellar
Because he is too fat;
He won't do any exercise,
He just lies on his mat.

I keep Santa in the cellar,
But elves smuggle him food in;
I'll have to change his venue,
How about the gym?

I keep Santa in the cellar,
But I'm going to let him go;
People are so cross at me
They miss his, 'Ho ho ho!'

He is *still* too fat!

Jessica Avery (11)

THAT GIRL WE ALL KNOW!

I'm looking down, I'm looking round
Just listening to that ridiculing sound
You may think I'm a drama queen
But really, honestly, they are that mean
I just can't keep it in anymore
It's slowly grinding me down to my core
I look around at other girls which makes me see,
How there are others just like me!
What gets me is they all have a friend,
You know, the one who's 'there till the end'!
Am I ugly or just sad?
Can I really be that bad?
Boys are just another chapter to my story
They find them hot whereas I find them gory!
I used to be popular but now that's gone
I thought I was pretty, and spots, I had none!
All of the girls just seek attention
Then they wonder why they get a detention
Is it just me, am I a fool?
Am I right to listen in school?
They think it's geeky, but it's how you achieve
They'd rather mess around and school they would leave!
And Facebook, that rotten site
Bullying starts overnight
This is not another rhyme,
About bullying, that horrid crime
This is for that girl you know,
Who's getting bullied by so and so
And when she gets so sick of life
She goes to pick up that kitchen knife
Let's make a change, let's get started
Be kind to her, be light-hearted
And then when you get old enough to look back at your past
You know that you brought her so much happiness just by making her feel first, *never* last!
So thank you for your time, thank you for listening
I know that with your help those girls who were hurt will be glistening!

Charlotte Pickering (12)

THE BIG M

Sometimes you are there
Watching me, silently watching me
I can sense your laser eyes searing into my back
Your eyes fixated on me, not letting go
Then suddenly you disappear and I can't see you
Like it was all a funny dream
But every day you always come back.

You trick me, tease me
Make me believe you're there
I actually think you're there and try to tell someone,
Then you're gone.

I can feel your hot breath on the back of my neck,
Hear you wheezing.
But I know it's not true.
You're not there and never will be.
But I remember every time I think you're not real,
That my family has been ripped apart,
Disappeared forever, just me left to hold the name
And I remember you're the big M I fear.
The big murderer.

Olivia Howe (13)

THERE IS A TIME ...

There is a time when you cannot speak,
Cannot breathe, a time to just stay silent.
A time of tranquillity, silence; musing about the future.
A time to live life to the full, to delight yourself.
A time to think about things never thought of,
A time to love and a time to hate.
A time to scatter stones and a time to gather them.
A time to gaze and a time to glance.
A time to devour the best foods and a time to fast.
A time to be embarrassed and a time to shine in the limelight.
A time to break and a time to heal.
A time to waste time and a time to treasure it.
A time for war and a time for peace.

Cassylda Augusto-Rodrigues (12)

LETTER TO YOU

Gaze at yourself in the mirror,
Brown, blonde, black hair,
Stare at your reflection in the water,
Green, grey, hazel eyes.

Talking to other people,
They see their reflections in your eyes,
Happy, sad, angry,
All these different expressions,
Seen by the same eyes.

You are funny,
You are dull.
You are popular,
You are friendless.

We love you just the same.

The gentle touch when you comfort,
A friend who is upset.
The feisty words you fire when you,
Get shot the middle finger.

You are unique,
You are common.
You are family,
You are a stranger.

We treat you just the same.

Darling, don't hate me,
We are alike.
Darling, don't love me,
You do not love me.

You are what you are.

The sullen soul hidden under,
The dazzling mind shown through your eyes.
The boiling emotions you feel,
The false statements others make of you.

You are what you are.

A beloved friend,
A familiar face,
A hated enemy,
A respected opponent.

You are what you are.

I accept
What you are.
And I expect,
The same from you.

Because, darling,
I am
What I am.

Xiyu Cheng (16)

PRIDE ROCK

How I'd love to be a lion
Sitting as the world goes by,
Sitting on Pride Rock
The view would never die.

How I'd love to be a zebra
Gasping at the view,
Gasping at Pride Rock
The view I'd share with you.

How I'd love to be a giraffe
Looking down at the world so high,
Looking down at Pride Rock
The world would run and fly.

How I'd love to be a monkey
Swinging through the trees,
Swinging over Pride Rock
The world a monkey sees.

How I'd love to be an animal
Watching the world and the view,
Watching over Pride Rock
I'd share the view with you.

Bethan Avery (9)

THREE LITTLE PIGS (AND THE BIG BAD SHEEP)

One day, the little pigs' mum
Said her body was getting numb
She finally said she couldn't live
With her grown and fat pigs.

She sent them out as quiet as a mouse
And whispered, 'Build yourself a house
You can jump and you can leap
Just please beware of the big bad sheep.'

'You can do a gymnastics show, roll and flip
Just race inside when he licks his lips.'
So off she sent her worried boys
In fact they were very annoyed.

One day they were out in their garden
The sheep turned up as a lady, 'Pardon
I'm very sorry, but I am in the mood for food'
The sheep did what the mother described
And the frightened pigs ran inside.

'I've just come to town so if you don't let me in
I'll huff and puff and I'll blow your house down.'
'No, I'm sorry sheep we aren't that thin, we won't let you in
For all the hairs on our chinny, chin, chin.'

Ellie Simpson (10)

STORMS

Lightning flashing,
Thunder crashing,
Darkness rolling in,
Children crying with their mums,
Babies hiding within,
Kicking trash bins upside down,
Howling down the street,
Mothers calling for their young,
To say it's time to sleep.

Jasmine Aldridge (10)

THE INFALLIBLE FIRST-WORLD

Tears slipping from her skeletal face,
The beauty of youth hastily escaping her as a dog retreats
Into its shell of shame,
From the owner whose hand sores their wet coat,
Eyes glistening with the gloom of blind ignorance.
But her eyes didn't glisten; they barely moved.

Her soft, fluttering eyelids forgot the face on which they lay,
Shaping the oval eyes in their coffin of blood
And pain which choked the innocent soul
That lay behind that yellowy-white shell.

Misplaced, her mother's gaze moved to the mystical
Mayhem now gracing her presence
With presents of consumerism and couch-potatoes
Caught in a world where 'help' is a trade, not a gift.
And she smiled,

A gesture encrusted with the golden cliché of Heaven,
Shadowed only by the beating sun on her raw shoulders;
Cold, in comparison to the fiery façade from which we came.
She had no idea, no burger or king,
No businesses singing to her empty pockets.
Her problems weren't solved by Google or Wiki,
No hangover Monday meant pulling a sickie.
Her life circled stomachs that shrink in the winter,
Not shrinks who solve our self-perpetuated depression.

And we stomach our privilege
With a spoonful of sugar,
Not knowing how our arguments fade
In a world full of pain,
Shown through a dying woman's smile.

Jennifer Evans (17)

THE POEM WITHOUT A NAME!

A great man once said:
'All the world's a stage, and all the men and women merely players'
We all play a part in life, which we shape into ourselves.

Etched onto us like a scar.
Life takes no prisoners,
We enter the world alone.
We leave the world alone.
Life is a game.
One played with both hands tied behind your back,
And the blindfold securely on.
No one knows where you're heading in life
Until you get there.
And when you get there it is like nothing you have ever experienced before.
Life is a mystery,
We are inadequate to see beyond the stars.
We live in our own bubble.
Our own world.
Prejudiced and biased, bursting at the seams.
We fail to live to the advances of our dreams.
We roll back down the hill when things get tough.
But I stand at the top of the mountain, burdened with stress and worry.
I stand and I look out to the land below me.
Living each day like there is no tomorrow.

Beth Wiggins (13)

SUMMER!

Summer, the hot scorching sun.
The smell of fresh cut grass.
The sound of waves crashing on the shore.
Hearing children playing on the sandy beach.
The smell of barbecues.
Hearing the tinkling sound of an ice cream van.
I love summer!

Orla Hughes (8)

FOREVER

It went on forever, they say
It goes on and on.
But how can that be,
Death will defeat us all.

He'll live forever they say,
The Doctor, he'll just regenerate.
But even he will come to an end,
After the last regeneration.

Forever they say,
A word with no real meaning.
It goes on and on they say,
But nothing ever does or will.

Forever they say,
Like waiting for the bus.
But that can't be,
It will turn up eventually.

Forever is a word,
A word of belief.
That gets the thought away,
The thought of an end.

'The story goes on forever,'
If it did there'd be no book,
And when everyone's gone,
Who will tell it?

Forever is a dragging word,
A shorter way of saying
On and on or never coming.

People think a poem
Should rhyme forever,
Or at least until the end
But the only rule in poetry,
Is always have a rhythm, a beat.

This won't last forever,
This is the last verse.
And you'll be glad,
This poem isn't a fad.

Damien Rist (17)

IT'S WEIRD HOW THINGS CAN CHANGE ISN'T IT?

Isn't it funny
That people are
So different to us (but in the good way) and also that it's
Weird that
Everyone has their own story
I for one have a very confusing yet
Really interesting one to tell
Don't leave just yet, I need to tell you my story

How to know of the interesting part started, well we'd have to go back in time
Oh how the screams were loud, the nights were long and how the glass looked sharp
Weird how things can change, isn't it?

Time progressed and the nights seemed longer and also
How time moved forward and how some people were held back
In there own world they have to finish there own story to tell, but they
Never get to see what was left of mine, the
Greatness I could and maybe one day achive
So see who decideds to stay and who decides to leave

Couldn't I be told earlier on that this was my story to tell
And is it possible for me to change the final chapter to my own book?
Never mind the past they say, it's gone, they say but who's 'they's' story?

Could you see me now, you would see
How I have grown and I am now less afraid of the loud sounds
And I hear less screaming, the nights are sometime shorter, and there's no more sharp glass
Never thought I'd be feel this way, never thought people would stay
Gosh I was wrong because people stayed, they knew my dark past and they stayed
Everyone has a story and they want to listen to mine, like how the lost boys stayed and listened
to Wendy

If you want to share your story I will
Stay and listen
Not leave you part way like Peter did or be the villian like Captain Hook is
To leave that would be rude because I have grown and I will not leave your story like he did

It's weird how
Things change, isn't it.

Rhian Louise Stowell (16)

A THOUGHT FROM ASH

Tongue of tempest that
Wreaths the flames,
Coiling and twisting;
Lost in names.

Soar does the phoenix,
Buffeted and blundered
By a tempest
That wondered.

Thought? An idea,
A candle flame, kindled
Against the icy breath
Of a wind, which dwindled.
Revelation.
The phoenix gleamed,
Like a teardrop of fire.
Its gold-scarlet plumage
Aburst in the pyre.

New life begins.
Stars erupt with light,
Blinding the darkness,
With all its might.

Petals unfurl, throats
Of deepest blue,
Which glimmer as the sun
Caresses the dew.

Wielding a weapon
No sword can match,
I take my pen
And release the latch
Of the mind.
The phoenix rises from
A stream of thoughts
… And is captured
On the paper.

Ahmed Aboukoura (16)

EXPRESS YOURSELF

Express yourself, my friend,
I'm telling you for your own good;
I'm telling you to save your soul
From the icy abyss where Identity is none.

Express yourself, my friend,
Scream into the starry night sky
And find yourself a home where
Your heart can say, 'Goodnight'

Express yourself, my friend,
Feel the fire in your belly
And throw it out your mouth
With everything you've got

Don't hold back a thing,
Don't hold back a sound...

Express yourself, my friend,
Hear the *power* that is spoken word
The spoken words of this spoken poet
Emanating from my chest.

Express yourself, my friend,
See the birds and the deers
See the scars and the tears;
See everything that is life.

Express yourself, my friend,
Don't fade into the crowd;
The sea of drowning people
All waiting till they wash aground.

Can't you see? Can't you see?
The people we are today mould
The people we will be tomorrow.
So express yourself, my faceless friend
You heartless hound in the howling hurricane
That is the virtual world we live in today
Because I can't see you I can't feel you
I don't know if you are real,

So express yourself, my friend
Let me know that you're alive
That you're breathing in the air
That I am breathing too.

Express yourself, my dearest friend
And let me know that you're you.

Daniela Sordillo (15)

WHO AM I?

Am I the guy who touched the sky?
Am I the guy who flew so high?
Or am I the guy who wondered why
I was living and dreaming in a world of sci-fi?

Am I the man who made slavery ban?
Am I the man who invented the fan?
Am I the man who, when given work always ran?
Or am I the man who puts the effort and always tries as hard as he can?

Am I the one who wrote this rhyme?
Or am I the reader at this time?
Am I one who must have his say?
Or am I the one who is called Shray?

Am I the one who found his way?
Out of the darkness of the day?
Have you ever asked yourself these questions and wondered why?
And then ask yourself, who am I?

Shray Khanna (13)

BROKEN LOVE

When I saw your face
When I saw the twinkle in your eyes
I was blinded by beauty
Why did you have to hurt me with all the lies?

Your sweet scent engulfed me in desire;
The feel of your lips on mine was too much to bear,
My heart raced every time you came within distance,
Every time I felt upon me your stare,
My knees went weak and my mind spun
Round and round and round,
As I started coming undone.

A surge of passion sprinted through my body
I lost all control as you kissed me
Your body was so close to mine
That you stole my innocent breath
For your touch so long I did pine
My heart used to beat for you
I lived to be held in your arms
My world revolved around you
You were the most important thing to me

When I found out the truth;
That you had betrayed me so badly,
Lied, cheated and humiliated me,
The pain in my heart (that once belonged to you)
It destroyed me, broke me, and tore me apart.
Every time I heard your name
I started burning up inside
I couldn't live surrounded by hurt and shame!

The regret and pain not only wounded me;
It damaged me to the point of no repair.
The scars you left will be a constant reminder,
How could you have an affair?
Anger, betrayal, distraught and destroyed,
The feelings of the moment my heart was crushed!

I trusted you with the power to break me,
And that is what you did,
I was a delicate and vulnerable rose,
You were the thorn that poisoned me,
The venom that plagued my heart,
Like a disease, a cancer,
That I allowed to taint my spirit, my trust in people.

Finally when I got past the pain,
When I started to heal,
Once my tears were no longer rain,
And the hurt was gone
I learnt to love again, to be happy once more
I trust him because I know that he won't hurt me.

Abigail Scollins (14)

A DAY IN THE LIFE

We go through periods of restlessness,
where the very air around us becomes stifling,
and not breathing has become more natural
than the act of breathing itself.
We drift through, walking like zombies on imagined clouds.
The beat of dead hearts keeping pace with the rough beats
on battlements and stone walls,
the rough and stupid wall around our minds.
We filter through distractions on a daily basis,
just to pass the monotonous moments of the day.
In which we struggle for any semblance,
of sense of self or body moulded out of brittle clay.
Together we are mismatched, broken body parts fitted wrong -
fitted onto a body that doesn't suit and blood that flows
in the wrong direction. Our bones ride the waves of red,
our souls have flown away to a better place.
There is no somewhere for us to go,
no somehow that realises hope and raises optimism.
Nothing but the rain in the clouds,
bursting over and over again to douse us with pessimism.

Chloe Kane (17)

LILLY

Lilly is the name of my 4-legged friend,
She's cuddly and furry, with a tail on her end.
She loves to go out during the day,
With lots of friends who love to play.
She's got nice soft paws,
Yet they contain dangerous claws.
She's black all-over, with a white tummy,
And 2 pointy ears which make her look like a bunny.
She is a Felix cat, with nice big eyes,
These can scare you at times.
No matter her mood,
She is always in for food.
I do dearly love her so,
I will never be able to let her go!

Maryam Hassan (9)

WITHOUT YOU MUM . . .

This is a poem dedicated to all the mums,
Who take care of us and fill our tums,
They always think about others and then themselves,
They always keep our rooms tidy and organise our shelves,
They go out to shop, telling us they just need a new mop,
And when they come back they bring along the entire shop,
When we're hungry they cook us food,
On the dining table they teach us manners, what's right, what's rude,
Keep us away from bad things like, drugs, beer and rum,
Make us look clever and others look dumb,
When our dad is about to shout at us she stops him instantly,
She tells us why we were wrong while she makes us some tea,
I can always stand by her as she's my best friend,
And this friendship is so close that it shall never end,
But when she argues with our dad she gets ready to leave home,
Says she'll book a ticket to Paris, London or Rome,
But when you're gone, without you Mum,
Who will take care of us and fill our tums?

Aman Rattan (12)

PUPPY

I've wanted a puppy for so, so long
I've pleaded and begged my mum.
I've wanted a puppy for so, so long,
But so far I haven't got one.

I don't mind what breed,
Small, big, quiet or yappy.
I don't mind what breed,
I'll let Mummy choose.

I'll buy it a lead, a bowl and a bed,
Just please let me have a puppy.
I'll buy it a lead, a bowl and a bed,
I'll walk it all the time.

I'll train it to do its business outside,
I pinky promise, I promise I will.
I'll train it to do its business outside,
You'll hardly notice it's here.

Perhaps my mummy will read this poem,
And finally change her mind?
Perhaps my mummy will read this poem,
Any my dream will finally come true!

Ashana Burford-Fleming

MY LIFE IN WORDS

My life was hard,
I was forever in a mard,
I had no one to talk to,
I didn't know what to do,
Until, the day I spoke up,
I told a grown up,
About the girl who always teased,
I dropped to my knees,
The relief hit me,
But she disagreed,
Had I lost or won?

Caitlin Pruhs Borrell (12)

LALALALA

She may not be the richest . . . she knows that.
She most certainly isnt the most popular . . . she's been bullied before.
She tries to hide her emotions . . . she struggles to cope at home.
She puts herself down . . . she wonders why she is alive.

But what she hasnt realised yet is that . . .

She is strong . . . she knows her weaknessess.
She is pretty . . . she is aware of her flaws.
She has a sense of humor . . . she got it from the sadness in life.
She is a loving person . . . she's experienced the hate.
She has no fears . . . she has discovered illusion from reality.

She is perfect to somebody out there . . . she just doesnt know it yet.

Rebecca Louise Speak (14)

IT WAS JUST A DREAM!

I walk nervously into an ancient room,
In there stands an old, rusty tomb!
I dare, want to have a look,
But I want to finish writing my ancient book.
On it I see that there is a key,
I wonder if one of the letters is 'T'!
I feel that someone is watching me,
It's making me so scared that now I need to go pee.
I hear a really loud scream,
All of a sudden I wake up!
I realise it was just a dream.
My next dream I have is about a little pup!

Maiya Stevens-Howe (10)

FLASH FLOOD

R   apid and wild, the untamable child.
I   nsatiable hunger, now feeding with thunder.
V   iolent power, her mission: devour!
E   xhausted, slow moving, her chase now defusing.
R   iver resuming, a pace that's approving,
S   o life begins blooming.

Amie Carter (12)

BEAUTIFUL IRELAND!

Stunning views as far as the eyes can see,
Magnificent fields green as green can be,
Sheep quietly grazing, horses galloping free,
Wheat, corn and barley blowing in the breeze,

Delicious food they love to eat,
Potatoes, stews, cabbage and meat,
Homemade cheese to go with the bread,
And everybody happily fed,

Laughing, smiling, having fun,
Dancing, prancing under the sun,
Singing songs, making tunes,
Drinking Guinness through the afternoon,

A wonderful sight, as the horses charge,
The crowds going wild as they gallop past,
The hooves like a drum with a steady beat,
Racing to the winning post in the heat.

Frankie Turnell (12)

NO WARMTH

The bench I'm sitting on is in remembrance of Paul Speller
He sounds like a builder, a joiner, and lived for 81 years
81 years of stairs for new houses, new homes.

And the leaves from the great trees fall into yesterday's snow
And as I lie adrift in my void of emotions
Shivers of feeling rush through my body.

Many people walk past me but do not look,
As if to mind their own business,
Or to not intrude in mine, to not look past the red jacket that covers me.

The sun shines but the clouds cover it
So there is a hot disk of yellow on the cold grey blanket of clouds
The blanket that offers no warmth.

Oscar Saharoy (11)

I WRITE THIS FOR . . .

I write this for the river, when the river bursts her banks,
I write this for the tree, when the tree sheds her leaves,
I write this for the wind, that howls in the night,
I write this for the moon, that is lonely and yet always in our sight.
I write this for the people, who leave us every day,
I write this for the strangers, who never seem to stay,
I write this for the seasons which come round every year
I write this for the dreamers, who succeed to follow dreams,
And I write this for the weak, who don't have the strength to follow,
Follow what they love, not just the highs that they borrow.
But most of all I write this, for the people who believe,
That with a little amount of courage, you have a chance to succeed.

Saskia Kershaw (14)

RUMOUR MILL

Trying so hard
To let it all out
Laughing endlessly through the aches inside
I can fake a smile
Force a laugh
To make you happy
But inside is the same
Empty, hurt
And waiting for an end
An end to the never-ending spinning of the rumour mill
So that I can be free
To spread my wings and have the weight lifted from my shoulders
And just for a while
I can be carefree
The spinning stops
Peace overwhelming my mind
I wait for the happy fairy-tale ending
Where it's all cheerful and peaceful at last
But the rumour mill keeps on spinning
Murmuring its daily song
A different tune every day
Taking me from my dream ending
My peace long gone
In the middle of the rumour mill.

Caitlin Harrop (13)

LIBERTY AND PEACE

Forced away from home,
Desperate to return,
To my birthplace.
Dragged into slavery,
And bondage held me fast.
Agony overwhelms me,
As I am tortured in anguish.
A life to live, though no life that I take pleasure in.
'Liberty' and 'peace' are what we deserve!

I want self-determination,
Determine is my name.
So why not join your faith?
And establish the 'liberty' that we deserve.
As we shout with confidence and conviction in our voice,
Why not grant us the liberty that is 'fair'?

Troubles here and there,
Troubles everywhere.
Bye to precious life lost in the wind.
For peace is here no more.
'Liberty' and 'peace' are what we deserve!

I want self-determination,
Determine is my name.
So why not join your faith?
And establish the 'liberty' that we deserve.
As we shout with confidence and conviction in our voice,
Why not grant us the liberty that is 'fair'?

This is our opportunity to stand for liberty
If we miss this chance, we're *gone!*

Henrietta Onyebuchi (10)

HERE ONE DAY, GONE THE NEXT

A tiger prowling through the jungle,
His amber eyes burning bright.
His orange coat and night-black stripes,
Shimmering in the strong moonlight.
But the poachers came,
So he was here one day, gone the next.

An elephant plodding through the jungle,
Making her way to the stream.
Her young calf grabbing her swinging tale,
Her eyes shining blue and green.
But the poachers came,
So she was here one day, gone the next.

An orang-utan swinging through the jungle,
Singing her way from tree to tree.
Climbing higher and higher,
To the place where they are free.
But the poachers came,
So she was here one day, gone the next.

A poacher strutting through the jungle,
His riffle at his side.
He spies a stealthy jaguar,
To take away and hide.
But the rangers came,
So he was here one day, gone the next.

Rachel May Smith (14)

145

A SPARK TO LIGHT THE HAY

Generations of anger flow as strong convection currents
Through the thick crowd.
Burning out. Regenerating.
The swelling glow of heat at the core of a hay bale.
With words thrown frivolously like the spray
Of waves smacking together,
The man hiding with a microphone mask
Wills everyone to stay calm
While he panics
Because everything he says is under control.

Frustration is inherited like eye colour,
Though we have our variations,
We can all see
And of what we see, we disapprove.
This unity is all we need.
A spark to light the hay.
In the alleyway rumours of rebellion
Rise to a fierce chant
And suddenly we clutch pitchforks in our savage fists
Wielding blades that shine lustfully for what we think is justice.

Stop, hush, we've shouted too loudly it seems.
Blue warriors rush in to capture us,
Shoot us down with torrents of icy water,
Diminish us to sodden lumps of hissing hay,
Silence us with our wrists behind our backs,
And tell us to go home, stay out of trouble and 'grow up'.

But when we do go home
Keeping our heads low to the ground with appropriate shame
We must listen to every parent,
Every teacher,
Every leader,
Every person who has ever ordered us to shut the hell up when they were talking,
Tell us to speak the truth,
With a barn ablaze in the background,
Even if our voices shake.

Vivienne Burgess (16)

WEEPING WILLOWS

Weeping willows compare to me;
The tearful dreariness, as blue as can be,
Leaves cold and white,
Snow falls through the night,
Constant tears; unique leafs,
Happiness is just a mere belief,
Death upon me in the lonely winters,
Belittling my thoughts to be as painful as splinters,
Each day we age,
Wrinkling like sage,
Not square nor plain,
But twisted and never the same,
Hollow inside,
Yet full of pride,
Trustworthy and bound into the ground,
It's a waste of breath when no one's around,
What is the life without moral and emotion?
Is it a consistent bad potion?
Or a hell brought upon us by the gods,
Whatever it is it's against my odds,
If I could wish upon a star,
I would make things better than they are,
It would lighten up my life,
The natural earth would become my wife,
Now you know what it's all about,
The reason I grieve with all my doubt.
But how could I live a normal life?
When I live with the devil's wife,
I get by each and every moment,
By praying through all the torment,
So remember tomorrow,
Forget today,
A mountain full of sorrows,
You can wash them all away,
When 'it' lures you into the dark,
Just hope and love you shall depart,
She plays her games and tricks,
Beware the demon shall strike back, quick.

Elishia Gaskell (14)

THE BLESSED HERO

In dark, muddy no-man's -land,
Lay the innocent; not the bad,
They didn't even know why,
They had to ruthlessly die,
The blood splattered corpses,
The mud covered corpses.

In the centre of it all a body twitched,
His head, he could only just lift it,
He stood up, with a mighty limp,
It was like he was bewitched to live forever, by an imp,
His uniform was muddy, yet easy to recognise,
This was British uniform, and though he was injured, he stood sublime.

'C'mon, David you can live!'
He said to himself, determined to stay alive,
'You haven't come all this way just to die you know,
Fighting the Jerries brought you here, that long ago.'
So David began his long journey home,
His leg was painful, but to take his mind off it he hummed a quiet tone.

David's story is a sad one, see,
Years before he joined the army,
A shell fell on David's home when he was out selling in the countryside from his fruit cart,
When he heard the news, he smiled faintly and said with a sad heart,
'I've lost my whole family you say, and that I have nothing to live for,
But I still have my job and my God that I still adore, and that I haven't lost in this bloody war.'

People asked why he wanted to survive and called him crazy,
He just smiled and showed them a picture with him grinning madly,
In the picture he was leaning on his cart,
Overlooking the beautiful countryside that he loved with all his heart,
The sun was blazing wildly,
'This is why, my friends, now you know that I love this country that God has given me, this is why.'

He was sitting in the remains of his home when they,
The army, came to make him a soldier and took him away,
This is when, the tragedy begun,
He had to leave his countryside which God had blessed him with to kill with a gun!
They had taken him away to train him in harsh conditions,
And because he was new he always had the worst missions.

But he prayed to God in every way he was taught,
And had always stayed alive in every battle he had fought,
The officers thought he was special and ranked him up,
And soon he was ordering them all, not cleaning with a mop!
But he had not forgotten God and if he had he would have died,
In this bloody battle, which no one had survived.

He was leading the charge against the Germans unwillingly, covering his weak spot,
And had lived for ages until he was surprisingly shot,
He felt his life coming out of him and with his last breath,
He said his last prayer and gave up to death,
But try as he might, he would not die,
And he lay there until the battle passed by.

This is where we have begun, friends, in the midst of this dark muddy field,
He walked and walked, still with a limp, till he could go no further, so he kneeled,
And lay down on his back, praying to God,
Soon a British patrol found him and took him to be treated,
David was as good as dead and asked God to end his pain,
Darkness fell and the sun turned to rain.

The Germans, mysteriously sent by God,
Cruelly talked and a shell they dropped,
Onto the hospital, David inside,
The clouds, they heavily cried,
The bodies, they were unrecognisable,
But David's glowed with holy light, like a hero from a fable.

In Britain today you can see his grave now,
On it, you can read it, but most was faded by rain, hail and snow,
It says; *David Walker. Died in hospital when a shell came down.*
David shall go down in history as the greatest man in town,
No! The world will remember him as the greatest young man!
And even though he has died, he will live with us always, from clan to clan.

Malak Mehdi (10)

MY FRIDGE

I was supposed to be going shopping with my mummy
But I was hungry and rubbed my tummy
I opened the fridge and looked inside
It smelled as if something had died
It looked like there was a sausage in there
 A banana, an orange, a pea and a pear
I saw something that looked like rice
But it could have easily been some woodlice
A pizza, a pineapple, some pasta, a boot
A mouse, a maggot, a mango, some old fruit
A cake, some coleslaw, a Coke, a book
A nail, a nappy, a nut, a fish hook
With all the food in there
I was so full I couldn't fit on my chair
I was full to the brim
I had no chance of getting slim.

Catherine Dickens (11)

THE CLASSROOM

In the classroom, I sat looking at the board.
Jen in the corner played with a pretend sword.
In the classroom, I went for a walk.
Tom was eating lobster with a fork.
In the classroom, I stood looking at the door.
Kelly was screaming and rolling on the floor.
In the classroom, I went bouncing a ball.
Mary had crept out and went to Meadowhall.
In the classroom, I was making a wish.
Sarah was jolly, eating a fish.
In the classroom, I was talking.
Sarah was busy walking.
In the classroom, I was having a weep.
Why did all this happen?
The teacher was asleep.

Amina Asad (11)

MAN IS HIS OWN WORST ENEMY.

You hunt us, man will kill us all for fun.
In fact I've never seen one so close, absent of a gun.
That night when the moon shone, soul-filling bright.
My heart slowly grew so dangerously tight,
As you shot my family one by one.

Trickling blood spilled,
While mourning howls filled the silent, emptiness of death in the air.

I studied those eyes; so hateful, so wide.
Foolishly hoping to find where his reason might lie.
Instead I found his gun pointed angrily between my own
But I knew if I ran I'd forever be alone.

I needed the endless pain to cease, I saw in his eyes
the confusion that flickered with my lack of scared movement.
His gun still clicked as my last thought ticked.

I am a wolf, proud of who I am, but man, don't you know?
My heart beats steady and my soul so true.
That's what separates me from you.

Kelsi Bowes (13)

THE SNAKE

As black as coal – an icy night,
It kills those folk, in its plight.
A scorching dagger in a battle of blood-shed,
The last thing seen is a shot of red.
The slit of the eye,
The pierce of the scream,
A life is what the snake will redeem . . .

Shenel Mushtaq (11)

GENERATIONS

Sitting here with my pen,
No knowledge on what to write,
I look up to the window,
And stare into the light.

Soon I sense I'm drifting,
Looking into my past,
Now I'll think of the future,
And the significance of the past

My father was a thinker,
As was his father too,
I myself – an academic,
And I know what I will do.

My mother was a musician,
Her music a joy to the ear,
Though that's not the path I have chosen,
For my later years.
That path belongs to my sister,

Skilful in music as well,
Though I know she'd be better,
If she didn't hide in her shell.

I will search the sciences,
For a key to unlock our potential,
Though that's hard with the current world's problems,
Both political and financial.

I wish to make this world better,
A brighter place before I die,
I want to show the human race,
Where its true love should lie.

For what will we do with our lives?
That is a question often asked,
While many people simply complain,
With the job they've been tasked.

But first we need a memorial,
Free of graffiti and desecration,
A place for people to remember,
About their past generations.

Aidan J O Collins (15)

TELL ME WHY?

I fought for you,
I cried for you,
I bled for you.

Yet you fail to know my name.

I haven't seen my
family in months!

Yet you still take yours for granted.

I'm hungry,
I'm starving,
Food's running low.

Yet you waste yours continuously.

I've never met you,
But I risk my life every day,
For strangers.

Would you for me?

Sometimes I wonder why I
ever wanted to be a soldier.

Maybe I should give up.
Why should I fight when
you don't care about me?

Why?

Georgina O'Hagan

NEVER GIVE UP!

No doubt, life is not a bed of roses,
No doubt, you are the victim of sorrow,
Do not regret for your misfortune,
Never give up your strength on the path of life,
Every struggle and hard work counts,
Your courage will lead your further path ahead,
Life has a new mystery every day,
Dare to face all hurdles in life which weakens your worries but not your hopes,
But still never give up your strength on the path of life.

Aisha Shoro (12)

DREAM FOR NIGHTMARE

Broken window shows each dream
Shattered lie you can't redeem
A wish upon a twisted heart
Diamond lie that ripped apart
Shards of truth a pane of glass
A broken dream that came to pass
A teardrop fallen in the rain
An unseen symbol of your pain
A silver thread upon the ground
Of lost hopes that couldn't be found
A web of lies and deceit
Twisted from each defeat
Bound by hatred from a flame
Burning bright, turning the blame
Blood red tears that fall right through
Showing all that wasn't true
A dream twisted to the end
A lie to truth from which you bend
A cold hatred from above
Back to silence shattered by love
A dreaming wish fallen from a heart
As each lie rips it apart
A teardrop falls from each eye
A wish that came in the form of a lie
Hopes that shattered upon the floor
Lies that were hidden behind a door
A dreaming eye that went unseen
Reliving everything had it been
A wish each year to have it sell
Your secrets that you can not tell
Hidden by all yet free to see
Each truth, lie, dream and wish as they be
To turn them back, a nightmare made
Losing battles, memories fade
And hopes and dreams are sold away
A lie born into a day
A reality turned back on you
From a truth they never knew
Careful all, for you will see
That secrets and dreams aren't safe to be
They take your dream, twist it around
Shatter the memories upon the ground

Whisked away by just one scream
They give you back your twisted dream
But when they do, this I tell
Your dream in exchange for a nightmare is what you sell

Rachel Newnham (13)

GOODNIGHT GRANDAD!

After you were gone,
I didn't know how to go on.
I would cry and cry,
And always wanted to be alone.

A day without you went on forever.
I couldn't see your smile or hear your voice.
A hole was made where you were,
And where you still should be.

After a year my life was still missing you,
The hole became bigger as life got harder.
I needed you there to make me strong,
To tell me that I'm still your little princess.

Now two years have passed,
And I can't carry on.
I need you to see what I'm doing,
I need to hear you say well done to me one last time.

Now this is where my message ends,
But I'm always here,
Waiting for the day when I can see you again.
So goodnight Grandad, I'll see you again someday soon.

Charlotte Hall

ALONE

I used to be lost,
But then I got found,
My heart is still broken,
Buried under the ground.

I don't know how to love,
'Alone' is my middle name,
Some people don't understand,
They think love is just a game.

They assume they have it all,
They think their life is figured out,
They will all be *so* happy,
Not a single little doubt.

Estelle Booth

Y. O. L. O.

The heavy smoke filled my lungs, engulfing my body
Coughing, spluttering, walking quickly past the smokers
Slowly killing their body
But then again *you only live once*

Screaming, beating, lashing out at your supposed loved ones
They're crying a piercing scream, that you have become immune to
Your conscience frayed, your family dismayed
But then again *you only live once*

Needles pierced into their bodies
So high they can't see the world crashing around them
Their savage smell masks their uneasy lives
But then again *you only live once*

But life isn't about that
It is there to love
Be loved
And spread love
Because *you only live once.*

Onyeka Obuaya (12)

156

MEDITATION

To relieve yourself of envy,
To relieve yourself of wrath,
To free yourself of any burdens that may be blocking your path,
To maintain peace of mind,
To remain true and kind,
To reach the place you most wishfully seek,
To say words that are wise when you speak,
To see things that are clearest clear,
To fight so strongly to get rid of your fear,
To live your life to the fullest extent,
To learn what responsibility actually meant,
To refresh your soul, body and mind,
To see things better as though once blind,
To achieve all of the above without a doubt,
Meditation is the answer, it's what it's all about.

Ishpreet Sundal (16)

CREATURE OF THE NIGHT

In the depths of all things dark
A perilous quest about to embark
Hunting down the great and good
No one would dare, but only one would
Creature of the night.

The Devil hides within everyone
And will not stop until he has won
But what is Heaven in this place so cruel
A place with no love, or mercy, or rules
Creature of the night.

As death brings the end
Life makes another bend
And as you take your last breath
I have brought another man's death
I am the creature of the night.

Emily Gough

CROC OR NOT

Today I saw a crocodile,
It sat and stared at me!
I didn't run, I didn't shriek,
In case I was his tea!

No move I saw the snapper make,
His jaws remained tight shut.
Whilst sweat poured down my forehead,
I heard rumbles from his gut!

I've been in worse predicaments,
But only in my head.
Like wrestling with big brown bears,
And monsters from our shed!

But feeling brave I shuffled close,
To see his scary jaws.
The crocodile was not impressed,
And flexed his giant claws!

The beast prepared to eat me up,
He snapped, he snarled, he blew!
But I just stood and tapped the glass,
Because this croc is in the zoo!

Wiilo Mahamed

A WONDER

Life is a fixed machine that breaks in the end.
Some of us, we forget we are living a 'life',
We lose our routes, our inner soul, our originality.
We forget we're a machine with an expiry date when first seen.
We are so intertwined with the luxuries and the delusory dreams.
We are lost, lost in this world as if we own it.
But I say, No! We certainly don't.
We're just gatekeepers of this wondrous world, in fact!
We are nothing, a lonely speck in this vast encompassing universe.
With a lost soul, who's unsure of its own being!

Sadaf Moosvi

TOMORROW NEVER COMES

You're coming home tomorrow,
I feel it in my bones,
And all the pain and death and sorrow,
Shall leave our houses and homes,

You're coming home tomorrow,
That is what I say,
So a new china set, I decided to borrow,
And by your empty bed I pray,

You were coming home tomorrow,
But tomorrow never came,
You're coming home tomorrow,
I have been saying again and again.

Hannah Hamilton (13)

A BATTLE

I lay coughing on my sick bed
Death shouting
Life whispering
I dozed off into an unknown world
I felt lost and trapped
This place was peaceful but lonely
A woman dressed in white came to me
A ray of sunshine followed
Suddenly a man in red appeared unnoticed
Thunder and lightning deafened me
Pressure filled me
My sins haunted me
My deeds warmed me
I felt desperation and regret
The man in red laughed at my discomfort
The woman in white placed her hand on me
She whispered forgiveness
Then I knew everlasting life was at my reach.

Cassey Ofochebe

HEARTBREAK

And I know that you feel pain but keep on smiling through
It's not tragedy until it's beautiful
This is too messy to ever be so pure
But it's truer than the realest thing to you.

It's all so small and self-contained
But it means the world to me
My heart is breaking and I swear that's not all
Because losing you isn't letting go a bit.

They walk on by and see the shadows
Of a long night's lack of sleep
But they don't know the truth behind
These misty clear-blue hazel eyes.

Teardrops and raindrops and snowflakes and sun
Moonlight sees secrets no one yet knows
Catch a breath and keep it safe
Because there's no kiss to keep you close.

Summer leaves the heat behind
Sweet-pea cheeks gleam anew
The moon and the tides are inconstant still
But the scars run deeper than any Fault.

Briony Butterworth

VOICES

They just come
I can't control it.
And when they do,
I lose all control; all senses.
I become scared and petrified,
Because I am a toy,
A puppet.
I am in their control,
And I have no say.

I try explaining to the best friend;
Why I'm hurting, how I'm hurting,
But the words never come out
So I leave it mid way.
I feel worse.
Upsetting the best friend,
Making promises that never end.
But I can't do anything,
Because I am just a puppet,
Under their control.

I hate them
I hate feeling this way.
So the sharp stuff comes out
And I cut away.

Aamna Shah (16)

WONDERFUL WAR

Bruised and battered,
Lives all shattered.
Muddy and bloody.
Blown to bits,
Men having fits,
And dying in pits,
What's gonna happen when the bomb hits?

Men march proud
And come back dead
Like slaughtered sheep
What a life they led
We call them heroes
That's all we know
We can't see behind their eyes,
Although, it is the window to the soul

Crash, bang, buzz and *boom*
The sound that will take us to our doom
Dirty, rotten, filthy trenches
They have to sleep in the gruesome stenches

They fall asleep
Not knowing if they'll wake
For some die in bed
And leave their painful ache.

Alaina Shafqat (13)

THE DANCE

United we stand and apart we fall,
Twilight fades and night calls.
A man stood upon an endless brink,
Thinking to jump, to fly or sink.

Ever he danced on the moonlit rim,
Where the shadows fall and hope is dim.
Ever he stepped from foot to foot,
Wanting to go and yet staying put.

Ever he dreamed of peace on Earth,
Where hope is found with love and mirth.
Ever he waited for his lover's embrace,
Who was joined with him in heart and grace.

His eyes were brown and his hair was long,
But ever he sang his heartfelt song:
'Where is my home, my hearth and door?
Where will I go when I dance no more?'

Ever he danced 'til his pale feet bled,
Ever he sang 'til his voice was dead.
No answer came and he fell into toil,
But his lover was true and her faith was loyal.

Her eyes were green and her hair was blonde,
And still she answered her lover's song:
'Your home is here, your hearth with me.
Your door ever stands beside the sea.'

He danced no more and she took his hand,
And led him to a peace-filled land.
'You have stopped your dancing, forever may it be.
And forever you'll stay, here with me.'

His hope was safe from evil's maw,
And against the moon he closed his door.
He had sung his song and shown his art,
And had, in the end, danced into her heart.

Bethany McTrustery

A NIGHT IN THE WAR

German bombers flying everywhere
Drifting silently through the air.

Sirens going off at night
Children hugging their mothers tight.

Buildings fall, fires alight
Dust and flames light the night.

The all clear alarm sounds
Another mess all around.

War is over, peace is called
So many men injured and mauled.

Britain will never be the same
All those soldiers who will never be named.

Carla Knighton

A PLACE

The world is a place
There's no one to rely on
It goes on unsafe
For everyone to die in

The closest will go
It bursts out inside you
The times that you love
Will burn, they won't guide you

There are people out there
Forgotten your existence
They won't ever be fair
To you or your companions

The world is a place
The beginning and end
It goes on unsafe
Until the very end.

Nayab Siddique

A SINGLE ROSE

There it stands so bold and strong
Alone in the wild it may stay long
Everything else has been long since gone
May the beautiful rose stay straight until after we're gone?

Things have died, the rose is still bright
The soil that surrounds the rose tight
Is brown and shines throughout the whole dark night
Protecting the rose, until it's gone it will fight

Its time has come to die
It will wither, petals will fly
Seeds will start their life elsewhere
The root will stay where it belongs
To remind us all of
A single rose.

Arooj Siddique

HARD LIFE

I go through a hard time,
I just sit in my room,
I throw things around,
Just to calm me down,
I know one day that everything will be alright,
But I am waiting for that day,
School is getting in the way,
And I am getting judged every day,
It's not fair!
It's time to get on with life,
Can I?
It feels like if I have been stabbed with a knife,
I don't know how I can go on,
When I look upon a shooting star I make a wish
But it always ends up in a swish,
I hope this is a fantasy
As I cannot endure this in reality.

Marrium Javed

165

GIVING UP IS NOT AN OPTION

Is there a future waiting for me?
Maybe if I just close my eyes and travel with my fantasy dream I wish to happen
A little bit taste of hope I could achieve
I am nothing more than a worthless piece of creation.

I give my best, I practise harder than yesterday
It's no work, nothing will work
I try hard, but my best just isn't enough
I couldn't give up, not now, not tomorrow, not ever.

My best I always give
'Not enough' you always say
I rise up, your words echo in my ear
My pain is too much, sorrow slowly appears.

Is giving up ever the option?
I never did hard work for myself,
I did it for you, to make you proud and for you to pay attention to me,
Giving up is not an option!

You want the best, but the best isn't really me
You expected too much, way too much
A mistake I made, worth a fortune you lose
I gain something, its worth nothing, but a disappointment

I have gone this far
To make you proud is halfway done.
Creation I might have been,
Worthless you might have thought.

The pain is paying off
My success is coming, I can see it
Just a smile on your face
Slowly painting.

I was then chill, I was confident
The finals will be over
Little by little I became hard headed
A 'failed' I receive.

You trashed me away from you
Been locked, and needed a punishment.
In a dark scary room I sat,
Shivers with cold, reflection of me in the past I see

A mistake I see
Not hers, not his, not theirs
It's me, my mistake,
A past that never can be done all over again

A future I dream.
Is there a future for me?
My fantasy to re-do it all over again.
Is there a chance to take?

Rowella Arellon

WATER

Water, water all around
Pitter-patter on the ground
Water falls from up high
Water falls from the sky
Splish, splash, splosh as it creates a puddle
Umbrella in a muddle

Whales splash, dolphins splosh
Water's what we use to wash
Water falls from tree to tree
Water falls in the sea

Water drips from a tap, disappearing down the gap
Water runs down a stream
Gathering together in a team
Water, water all around
Pitter-patter on the ground.

Beth Templeton

SILENCE AT THE END

The room is silent
A hallowed turtle shell
The fire leaps up like a leopard
The smoke begins to smell
The wall paper melts made of wax
Paste falls from the ceiling a lava hail
The house is alight, burning bright
The wood is weak and frail

The Thames water bursts the pipes
An attempt to help the frail burning body
The heated metal pot with a cutlery sail
Rejecting the waters help
The weak legs just fail
Crumpling into its self

The house is flattened mail
The fire drains and leaps up again
Skate boarding across the balcony rail

In search of another house to devour
In all its power

Silent nightly hour

Rachel Ogunbayo

EYES THAT WERE TO ENGULF HIM WITH GRIEF

That day a fox came
But he never dared to show himself;
He lingered in the darkness of shadows
He waited near the orderly meadows.

The following day, the fox came; silent like the night
Yet this day he urged forward – waiting purposefully.
Under the coniferous tree, he found his shade.
He waited once again, till the sun in his eyes began to fade.

Near pastures of green, his eyes followed,
Where they saw, the waters flowing with tranquillity,
Rush, swoosh, shush the soothing sounds, filled his ears.
And he murmured quietly, anointing his heart with fears.

As night drew on, he raised his head,
Searching cautiously, smearing his heart with fears.
There from the wilderness came a cry,
And deep inside his troubled eyes, the sound became arid.

Trees swayed frantically, uprooting many in the process
Winds lashed out, sweeping the mountains
With heavy rain thundering its way, ripping the skies with darkness
Lurking through the green, the fox felt eyes – eyes that were to engulf him with grief.

Joshitha Mathew

INSPIRATION

A dark, dull, shapeless face stands there at the doorway, collapsing like a pyramid of cards. The person I most admire, the (now destroyed) figure most important in my life.
My aunt.

'I'll put you to sleep,' she used to coo, when I feared the evil monster that would jump out from beneath my bed at night.
Her soft, silky hands would gently stroke my hair and her eyes – caramel mousse – would smile down at me with tender love and affection, assuring me that the silly monster didn't exist.

'I'll put you to sleep,' I whisper quietly in her ears while my eyes penetrate through her deep grey eyes, closing like a shutter on a camera – taking the last picture it can save in its memory.
Tears avalanche down her cheeks as she whimpers in pain like a helpless baby, because of her useless kidneys.

'To the beach!' she shouted ecstatically two years ago . . .
We drowned ourselves in sweet, strawberry ice-cream and sat a ruler's width away from the salty sea water, enabling it to lick our feet clean and continue lapping our bottoms, like a dog laps his owner's face.

I push back the salty water in my eyes as well as the beautiful memories and stroke the layer of skin above her bones.
Perfect for a brail reader: bumpy, wrinkly and rugged.
Like balsa that hasn't been smoothed with sand paper yet. No moisture.
My pupils pierce into her skin and absorb the dirty blue complexion.
It doesn't blush a rosy pink anymore. No radiance, no life.
Just an uneven road . . .

Your lips have formed a dry, crusty, white skin on top with a crimson crack running down the centre. I see blood attempting to escape . . .
It can't. You have no blood. You have no bliss.

I really do admire you for enduring the pain you are experiencing.
As the blood pumps up and down (in the plastic tubes they sew to your arm every time you do for dialysis) you glue yourself to the hospital bed for six hours every day – without complaint.
Do I look up to you for inspiration?
No. I look up to you the way you look up to Jesus and pray that someday, the voice that my eardrums used to dance to, the eyes that used to smile like a crescent moon, the kiss that used to warm me up, will come back!
Will come back when someone donates their kidneys to you . . .

Nadia Chowdhury

MY VIEWS ON POLITICIANS

We live in a world
Were money is the motive
We vote politician in
Then they forget about the voters
Were in the dark
Lighting up candles
Around 389 MPs
Have the cheek
To commit scandals
A couple of months ago
I read 'Animal Farm'
With one of the best teachers
And guess
What was amazing about that teacher?
In couple months he got us
Teenagers
Reading and having our own opinions
My opinion is
I believe that politicians are no
Better than creatures
We live in a society
Were we're pushed to one side
Where kids join gangs
And die violently
Where facing cuts
50,000
Doctors, nurses, midwives
To lose their jobs
That's nuts
Why should we pay for?
The mistakes that
The government make
Why should we pay?

Hayat Ibrahim

THE BUSIEST CITY KNOWN TO MAN

People selling goods all over the street,
Visitors, citizens, all kinds of people you meet,
The streets of the city are covered in,
Churches and cathedrals, you'd better not sin.

This place is beautiful, beautiful but mad,
Motorbikes are everywhere, annoying, just a tad,
Beep, beep, car horns, enough to give a fright,
This even carries on all throughout the night.

Like the rest of Italy it's a famous place to eat,
Ice cream, pasta and pizzas are treats,
The restaurants are lovely, easy to find a few,
You can go for gorgeous risotto anywhere too.

Piazza Navona, stalls selling art,
Different kinds, modern and old, but all are on a cart,
Trombone, trumpet, music fills the air,
Hustle and bustle, people everywhere.

Spanish steps - amazing sight,
Always fantastic throughout the night,
And in the day the place to be,
Are the Spanish steps in this city.

The Swiss Guards' uniform makes them look like clowns,
As they guard the Pope in the Vatican town,
In the museum is the Sistine Chapel,
And a picture of Adam and Eve eating an apple.

Lovely place to be, St Peter's Square,
Click, click go the cameras, people everywhere,
Enormous pillars standing in perfect lines,
The Basilica is open to groups of every kind.

The Pantheon building tall, huge and great,
Built for gods and to celebrate,
Buried within is Victor Emmanuel two,
Surrounded by places to eat nice food.

Roman ruins lie all over the floor,
Nobody could possibly ask for any more,
The Colosseum towers above everyone,
Can you believe it is not all gone?

More Roman ruins ruined even more,
Though long time ago they wouldn't have looked like this I'm sure,
The name for this place is Palatine Hill,
All the things are beautiful; your dreams they must fulfil.

Trevi Fountain's water leaps out fresh and cold,
Everywhere the statues beautiful and old,
Throw a coin in you'll come here again,
Busy with all races, women and men.

Now I have named famous buildings - eight,
This city stays awake till very late,
Begins with R and ends with E,
Can you guess? It's Rome city!

Bethan Law

A NIGHT IN LONDON

Waiting for the bus, I fear,
A midnight stranger might come near.
I tremble, I cry, I laugh, but how,
I should be home by now.

People bustling here and there,
'Please sir, money for the bus fair?
I must be back at my home,
But I can't, I'm all alone!'

There isn't a bus in sight,
It gives me a large fright.
At home they're eating liver,
How I wish to be there.

This is Victorian London.

Florence Balcombe

LOST AND FOUND

There once was a house,
On top of a hill,
The owner had left,
'Cause he hadn't paid the bill!

But inside this house,
And under the bed,
A small teddy lay,
'Cause he'd banged his head.

His tummy was ripped,
His arms were torn,
But he had been loved,
And was very worn.

The owner had liked him,
But left him behind,
Purely because,
He was almost blind.

The teddy climbed,
And sat on a chair,
'I know what to do,
I'm such a clever bear!'

The day before,
He had overheard,
His owner talking about,
Going abroad!

He raced outside,
And down the hill,
Through the farm,
And past the mill.

He ran to the airport,
And jumped on a plane,
He flew across France,
And ended up in Spain!

Tired and exhausted,
He stopped at an inn,
Where he saw his owner,
Searching in a bin.

The owner looked up,
And could just about see,
His lost friend Ted,
'Why this just can't be!'

'There you are!'
Teddy cried,
'I've found you,
After I tried and tried!'

'Teddy, it's you!
Take my hand and don't let go,
We're together forever,
Oh, how I love you so!'

Tabitha McCartan

BOOKS

Lots of pages fixed together
Makes a golden book together
And if you're lucky enough to find
A golden book of nursery rhymes
Swords and armour
Shields and knights
In a castle
In a fight
Cinderella leaves a shoe
A fairy says to her, 'Go, shoo!'
Tick-tock goes the big grand clock
Here comes the prince to help all of you
Penguins dance with their feet
Sing and dance and have a feast
Look at all these lovely books
Read one and it will . . .
Help you too.

Chineme Iloh

NEW BEGINNING

It's only the beginning now
a path yet to be known
sometimes life can end in sorrow
but we shall never walk alone

Memories still within
sometimes I wonder if life will give me a blow in the head
life could be frightening
as a new one could fall to its darkest hours

Part of our lives are not always joyful
moods often fall low
the shadow our lives leave behind
is the promise of its glorious day

New beginnings will come; old beginnings will go
today I will run, tomorrow I will walk
it's time to start fresh and make a broad smile
so it's time to forgive and forget

I do not accept the boundaries
and pressures from the past
I free myself of all prejudice
and hold values that last

God allow me to make the right decisions
and teach me to use my time
to accomplish my greatest goals
and to strengthen the life of mine.

David Aladesuru

??????

Viewing up into the dark sky
All light is shining in my eyes
I remember what this is all about
And here is my story about my excruciating life

It all began with one single knife
How I was so stupid to keep it as my possession
But what can I do? I'm isolated in a world of crimes
I wander through the midnight forest
Wondering how I'll keep up with my world upside down
Until I reached the desolated lake
The forceful wind twirled round me
Enveloping me
There it was, my reflection on the lake
Gazing in to my eyes

A shadowy figure was behind my shoulders
What is it? Where did it come from?
From behind a hand seized me
It dropped me on the floor
Simultaneously kicking terribly hard to free my self
Conflict in my soul
I just couldn't
Should I give up?
Die or
Be strong.
I breathed in the scented smell
He's probably a nefarious grave digger
The lost soul hung around him.

Sabrina Belaziz (12)

JOURNEY

We walk down our roads
Through our wondrous journeys
We take whatever life throws
All the time learning

We stumble, we arise
Some grow wise
We tell truth, we tell lies
We love self or empathise

We stand tall and proud
We are quiet, we are loud
We are slow, we are fast
Our memories die, our memories last

We fight, we back down
We smile, we frown
We work, we play
We move, we stay

Our lives our short
Time runs fast
Make the most of your journey
Make every moment last

We breathe day and night
We bleed, we feel pain
We see, we are blind
Always we develop our mind

We leave we arrive
We look to survive
We accept, we deny
But in the end we all die

Ashley Singh (13)

DEAR ANGEL

Drift towards me, dear angel,
Float on clouds of dreams.
Engrave them onto paper,
And thread them in my ear.

Preserve each one, dear angel,
So it can travel the world,
So people like me, the patient,
Gather wisdom from your words.

Drift towards me, dear angel,
Wrap me in your wonderful ways.
Weave your lessons into my life,
Sprinkle your love on me.

Show me pain, grief and loss.
Give me joy, love and peace.
Be gentle, dear angel,
But be harsh to me too.

Drift towards me, dear angel,
And show me your face.
For each angel is a writer,
And they wrap their thoughts with lace.

They push them into poems,
And into stories and books.
They are so unpredictable,
You're kept on tenterhooks.

So drift towards me, dear angel,
Set your words to sail.
Sit by me, dear angel,
And tell me, your tale.

Olivia-Savannah Roach

HALF-DEAD HERO

I hear groans of pain in the battlefield,
I sometimes wonder, I really do,
Why don't lazy men see the message?
It's everywhere on the streets,
Is it just that they are too scared,
Or don't want to be much of a hero?
I get no reward for being in the war,
Just broken bones and limbs.

Right now I see dead bodies of soldiers,
Surrounding me as I hear gunshots,
Trying to aim towards me,
My rifle is swung across my shoulder
I am ready,
It's turning dark now,
I see silhouettes of my enemy,
I shoot but then again so does my enemy.

It's hard to see which bullet is mine,
But I see a bigger bullet coming towards me,
I dodge but not quick enough,
The bullet goes straight through my brain,
And all I remember is that I'm not just a half-dead man,
But I am a half-dead hero.

Sumayyah Haseeb

SKINNER

He is as kind as a tooth fairy
He is as strong as a giant crocodile
He is helpful and forgiving
He is as peaceful as a new summer's day
He is Mark Skinner

Rosa Littlewood (6)

MY CAT OSCAR

He came to us a small bundle of fur,
He followed us around and often purred.
He looked so cute with his big, green eyes,
But missing his mummy he often cried.
Now that he's a fully grown cat,
He just lies by the fire slowly getting fat.

Not interested in catching birds or mice,
He would rather be sat on someone nice.
His name is Oscar, a long haired tom,
And I would miss him if he were gone.

Eve Catherine Jones

WITHOUT THE ONE

Without the one
There is no train,
For some precious part is missing.
And so they travel alone.

Without the one
There is no food,
For some ingredient is missing.
And so they dine alone.

Without the one
There is no fun or hope or joy,
For some feeling is missing.
And so the whole is broken.

But in years to come
They won't learn
That there is no Earth
Without peace.

And so the wars go on.

Pandora Mackenzie (11)

ODE TO IRELAND

Celtic Tiger, fierce and bold,
Leprechauns with pots of gold
A courageous country, proud and true,
A valiant emerald in a sea of blue.

Hunger took you hostage in 1845,
Weathered by weakness, few would survive.
Times were tough; money was tight,
Cause of this problem? The potato blight.

Belfast's finest built the boat,
1912 set Titanic afloat,
An iceberg sank the captain's dreams,
From the depths of the sea, those drowning screams.

Fields so green; the Emerald Isle,
The farmers harvest with a smile,
Pristine in pine, the trees stand tall,
Waiting for autumn to harvest them all.

Irish dancers, the best I've ever saw,
The beat of their feet leaves the crowd in awe!
Their dresses, like rainbows, light up the room,
Dancing, they magically follow the tune.

Celtic Tiger once stood tall,
But after pride their comes a fall,
The tiger now has lost its bite,
But we shan't rest 'til things are right . . .

Sarah Comiskey

HOW I FELL INTO THE RIVER THAMES

Along River Thames, I walked
the water swished, swashed and rocked
the long boats docked
nature so beautiful, my eyes were locked

I fed the ducks in a glade
oh what a noise they made
with them as I played
in the path a little I swayed

Thud! I fell with a trip
in the river I had a dip
as I started to shout
Mummy pulled me out.

Shriya Kashyap

SHE LOVED TO READ

She sat in the corner and stared into space,
Her heart and her mind she forever did chase,
The absence of caring caught hold of her soul,
As the teacher droned on about life protocol.
Maths was alright and English okay,
(Except for times when homework was an essay)
But she longed for that freedom found only in books,
Those times you escape all the judgemental looks.
She longed for adventure with pixies and imps,
With unicorns, fairies, zombies and chimps.
So when the bell went to end the school day,
And the children all left to go out and play,
She went to the library and didn't yet leave,
It was her safety, her home and reprieve,
An escape from reality, an escape from the noise,
To read all the books that she truly enjoyed.

Bethany Nelson

HOLY CROSS RIOTS, NORTHERN IRELAND 2001

Don't confine me into corners – stop forcing me to fight.
Don't brand me with a stereotype,
This world ain't black and white.
I wasn't born under a tricolour,
I wasn't christened with a flag,
So just 'cause I live down South Way,
It doesn't mean I'm an IRA slag.

This sectarian divide; this carving of our streets,
This paramilitary violence,
You're forcing pathways for my feet.
Do you remember Ardoyne Way?
Have you traced the red brick of Wailing Wall?
Do you hear the echos of vicious catcalls,
Where I walked my way to school?
Blonde hair parted with two ribbons,
New grey skirt brushing the knee, Being herded through bestial riot shields,
Having urine, hatred, half bricks hurled at me?
Mam covered rose-blush ears,
Shackled me firm in place,
As I tripped dazedly up glittering tarmac,
Cold tears swallowing freckles on my face.

This orchestrated anger – a cacophony of cries.
I could see you in their faces,
I stumbled the gauntlet of your eyes.
Crowds surging; hissing, spitting, snarling,
Ten green bottles that shredded the sky,
This tidal wave, a roar of insults,
Sobbing, 'What for Mam – why?'

Ten years later I touch graffitied brick,
Close my eyes, smell petrol, hostility, fear.
Half bricks and broken glass still litter the shadows,
What terrible things did happen here?

Blue sky, grey skirt, community, identity,
Red brick, green bottles, sadness, enmity,
Rose-blush ears of things that could have been,
If civil blood hadn't made civil hands unclean.

Emma Maynard (15)

DECAY

Memory,memory you fade away,
like the clouds in the sky you never stay,
and as time passes you want to say,
oh please, don't burn or corrode away.

Oh, memory oh,memory,
the painful and happy times will never wither,
the scars and the traumas we hope will waver,
for a happy life to look forward to,
don't look behind to the painful ones,
look and copy the joyful ones,

Oh memory oh memory
as you fade,
I'd like to say,
I'd like to swear,
you've helped me cope,
and you helped me bear the tough and the overwhelming times.
oh, memory, oh ,memory.

Chloe Parsons

MY FIRST POEM

As soldiers fight so hard and brave,
Which country will win or fight to their grave?
They tremble with fear and deadly sweat,
Who will win that harmful bet?

The war, that war, it never ends,
I wonder when we'll all make friends.
The swords and daggers slice through bodies,
This can't be their real hobbies!

Nearly all men are finally dead,
The women have no one to wed.
We will run away, it might be OK.
We run for dear life all day.

Lily Victoria Gregory (8)

ALIVE

It's just no good, no good at all.
My life of sadness, the way I fall.
My leaps and bounds, and falls and sounds,
My wrecks and tumbles, right on the ground,
The clime of life, to fall at the peak,
The light in my eyes, stole from the weak.
The space in my soul, the hole in my brain,
Been shot out again by the driver of sane,
My reality weak; it starts to shut down,
To see ideal, beginning to drown.
Too many days, where life can seem still,
But times when its moving, my heart stops at will.
The times that I breathe, to stay right up high,
I can't tell my parents, can't break down and cry.
But please don't worry, my friends tell me so,
And yet I see laughter, they stop yet they go.
My wanting is over, only know to survive,
But time and again, I hate the verb of 'Alive'.
And God and Jesus should be set in my mind,
But when I fall down again it's a hate of mankind.
So I crack out my pen, I begin to write,
My story, what I am; my love is in the night.

Jacob Seelochan

MEMORIES

He's small and black with glowing eyes,
He always smells of the garden,
And when I wake up I hear the
Cries of hunger.

But that's just Gordon Brown.

I can't even begin to count the amount of times I have
Shouted at him for scratching the chairs,
And scaring the fish, or even when he kills the birds and
Frogs.
My cat is different like that you see.
His favourite toy is a tied-up crisp packet.
All my Gordon does is eat, sleep and cry.
He jumps at his own shadows and runs from the guide
Dogs
And people who aren't usually in the house all the
Time.

But that's just Gordon Brown.

Bethan Radburn

BLOOD ON MY HANDS!

It was a cold summer's evening,
The end of the day was looming,
The evil of the nightlife was ready for work,
Tuck your children up in bed,
Safely rest your weary heads,
Wake up with blood on your hands,
The evil has had a busy night.

Lauren Schofield

IT WAS SO QUIET THAT I HEARD . . .

It was so quiet that I heard . . .
The gentle whirring of somebody's brain
It was so quiet that I heard . . .
The short, sharp buzz of a fly hitting the radiator
It was so quiet that I heard . . .
Leafcutter ants slicing through leaves
It was so quiet that I heard . . .
Telephone conversations whizzing through wires
It was so quiet that I heard . . .
The trees whispering softly, telling secrets that only they know
It was so quiet that I heard . . .
The slash of a blade as Henry VIII executes his wife, Anne Boleyn
It was so quiet that I heard . . .
The splash of William the Conqueror's ship as he invades England
It was so quiet that I heard . . .
The Statue of Liberty scratching her head
It was so quiet that I heard . . .
Nothing!

Lauren Stewart

WHO CARES?

Nobody cares about me,
I'm only a child, you just can't see,
I've been beaten, tortured and raped,
Nobody can relate.

I'm just a piece of gum on somebody's shoe,
Nobody looks after me,
For my appearance is not as it seems,
For like everyone else, I have dreams.

I've been scratched and stepped on,
On the test of destiny, I never won,
I guess I'll always live my life like this,
Until my death, ended with a fist.

Hydea Makayla Thomas

BECAUSE YOU ARE MY MOM . . .

Because you are my mom you loved me before I was ever seen
You thanked God for this miracle, this little human being
So exciting, yet fragile it all must have seemed to you then
Hearing my little heart beat inside you, now life begins.

Because you are my mom, no pain was too great for you to bear
Now you're a mother and I your child, with joys and pains to share
And so into this world my life began, each breath now on my own
One day we will look back at just how much I've grown.

Because you are my mom you worried for me within your every bone
You finally let go of my little hand to take my first steps on my own.

Because you are my mom you showed me through the years
To care about others and their feelings and the things that they hold dear.

Because you are my mom you taught me right from wrong
Understanding that my *faith* in God will forever keep me strong
Showing me that being my own person is the only tool I'll need
When morals and values are your foundation to succeed.

Because you are my mom you loved me enough to also be my friend
You would be right there in ways that no one could see or ever comprehend
When there was no way I thought you could ever understand
There you would be, non-judging and willing to lend a hand.

Because you are my mom, God's gift to me was you
As your daughter I will always love you and promise to be true
I thank you for so many things and will try to never make you sad or blue.

Because you are my mom, and one day I will be a mother too
I pray I never forget all that you've been through
I am your daughter and in your image I am proud to be
By the grace of the Lord you were created, and then I came to be.

Niharika Mathur

I CAN'T WRITE A POEM

I searched and racked my brain,
Looking for a ditty.
But the words just won't come,
It's really quite a pity.

The pen to the paper,
Is off it and on it.
As I strive to derive,
The perfect eight line sonnet.

I've tried enjambment,
And personification too.
But when it comes to poems,
I don't have a clue!

I'm starting to doubt,
My high-scored IQ.
As I can't even grasp,
The rules of Haiku.

I try to write,
But the words just get muddled.
It's very frustrating,
And I'm rather confuddled.

Scribbling out lines,
The words just don't go.
And it's all rather odd,
The process is slow.

At last, I've got a title,
I'm hitting my stride.
I'm an Olympic sprinter,
I'm surfing the tide.

I'm exploring a jungle,
I'm flying to the moon.
I'm stroking a cheetah,
I'm in a hot air balloon.

I'm climbing a mountain,
I'm at a zoo.
I can do anything in the world,
I put my mind to.

Sorry . . . I can't,
It was all just a lie.
'Cause I can't write a poem,
And it's making me cry.

Danielle Watts

FINIS ENTITY

The future belongs to those who
believe in the beauty of their dreams.
but she's trapped, inside the prison walls
her mind incomplete.

Plagued with emotions
the days she disappears
emptiness fills, her eyes
as fragments from her past
float by.

despite her shadow's
presence
tuneless is the song
some say it's living death
I disagree
she's more alive
than she could ever be.

Tahmina Shakil

UNTITLED

As I looked out of the window,
I saw the dark sky.
Sensing it was going to snow
I cuddled up and went to sleep.

The snow had started falling,
Flake by flake to the ground.
Oh! How beautiful it was,
To see the snow build up in mounds.

The weather became freezing,
Everyone was shivering.
Oh! What a nasty temperature drop there was,
With all the cold, cold snow.

But how elegant the snow was falling,
As if in a ballet dance.
Each flake danced a rhythm,
Swaying and moving from sound to sound.

I could not believe my eyes,
When I saw the snowflakes dancing.
I knew it was a dream of some kind,
But no, it was all real.

I slipped on my tunic,
My hat, my socks and mittens.
I went outside the house,
To understand all the happenings.

Suddenly the snowflakes,
Seemed to freeze when they saw me.
As if they were icicles,
Not swaying or moving at all.

I told them not to fear me,
I was a friend of theirs.
Then they started moving,
Dancing, swaying and all.

The snow had made a seat for me,
On which I was to sit.
And watch the beautiful snowy show,
As the time passed, slow and slow.

It was almost daytime,
The snow had started to melt.
Oh! What a sad ending,
To such a lovely show.

I sneaked back into bed,
Promising the snowflakes,
That I would never forget them,
Their moves and the show.

I woke up with a start,
Thinking it was a dream.
I rushed down and told my mother about it,
And she said, 'What a lovely dream you had.'

Ishani Mohit Udas (10)

IN PRAISE OF YOU

Tears drop from my eye
Which has keenly seen you when you said, 'Goodbye'
Doesn't the same happen to you?
Or has your eye been sewn by a grand cloth adorned with jewels and dew?
How the past was nice!
When we were just like scurrying mice
Creeping with joy and like mad
And my taste was just as your fad
High calibre you only at times err
You're my dream fairy with wings of golden fur!
Your presence wasn't just a sight of might,
It's an odour filling rusted hearts with glee
Which gripped me when I wished to flee.
You consoled me when I wore a scowl
Just as a brilliant white owl
. . . Now why desert me
When my eyes wish fervently you to see?
. . . Yes, now I accept it - thick or thin, green or yellow
All shady trees of knowledge,
When time calls, shed their foliage
Still dear friend, you continue to be a golden letter of my eternal memory pages
And one of the best unknown sages!

Atique Munaf Mallabadkar (18)

ANGELS

The night was dark; darker than most,
The guards in their armour asleep at their posts.
The angel looks down with a hollowed-out face,
Feeling the dread wind around the dark place.

Seemingly worlds away another one stands,
His mind idly swimming through thick seas of sand,
Hearing the silence that he did most fear,
Straining for the footsteps that he longed to hear.

Word got around fast, that the angel was sick:
The roaring of words were just as thick,
As the tears that followed deep down inside,
When the phrase took the man quite by surprise:
'The angel is sick! The chances aren't good!'
Cried the messenger grim, his words to chill blood.

Down the hall he ran,
The man in the white,
With the deep, dark hair and eyes immortally bright.
From one room to another and through those big doors,
Into the room with the wooden floorboards.

The room was as dark as the hall outside,
Though lit with the glow of a candle at the side,
Of the big, wide bed where the angel did rest,
Sunken eyes closed and hand upon breast.
Hair that was straight, long and white,
Silver skin that looked dead in the light.

Dead the angel was not, but soon would be,
As death sidled down the corridor, as quiet as could be.
The angel saw him coming, from past the thick walls,
Past the black night and through the great doors.
Turning their face they opened their eyes,
Looking up at the man with the lips and the lies.

'Don't leave me now,' said he, before the angel spoke,
'Not after everything,' and the words sorely poked
At the angel's soft heart, so warm and sincere,
'Because I love you, I swear, and I don't want to hear
The voice of the bells as they ring in the steeple,
Ringing the news out to the people
Of your death, my love, so please don't give in:
If you keep on fighting, then maybe you'll win.'

A smile was mustered upon the angel's face,
Falling, falling, through the space
Between life and death, forever descending -
Death will be here soon, my life is 'ere ending.
'This isn't your fault,' the angel said,
'It never will be - and this isn't the end:
You know I'll be watching you,
I'll always be watching you.'

Then followed a silence, so deep and true,
That the man could just stare at the angel's light hue,
Angelic demeanour, silver and white,
Like a frail skeleton draped with moonlight.
Tears did not fall, no disturbance at all,
But the angel could see Death wandering down the hall.

Hurry! The angel cried out in Death's mind,
Take me from here! Just let me die!
In the short time the angel had left,
The angel reached out with a touch almost as cold as Death's,
And touched the man's face, the one so cherished,
It was all the sick saw as they slowly perished.

'I love you, I love you, forever I will,
So don't forget me – please, don't forget me.'

Death entered then, as silent as night,
And the man did not see him, for only the angel might,
Be able to see Death's hollow eyes,
As the demon approached and reached the bedside.
The angel looked up with calm, flattened eyes,
Which were merely a blue and warm midday sky.
You know this, my angel, that I am here to take you,
And you must leave him: he cannot go with you.

The angel looked at the man kneeling beside the bed and held a steady gaze,
Smiling slightly with a tired face and eyes full of haze.
Death slowly reached down with frozen hands to claim the angel's life
And the man watched, paralysed, as he saw the light,
Fade from the angel's eyes and slowly did they close,
And the pale hand once on his face fell down to the bedclothes.

Bella Saunders

195

AN EQUAL WORLD?

I heard your thoughts yesterday, for a new world,
You know, you're a dreamer but that's not enough.
I saw your eyes crying, for a change to happen,
But the world today, it is as it was yesterday.
I read your lips, as a child was dying,
Until now, another fifty have crossed the other side.
I saw your throat swallowing just a small crumb,
And I stood laughing because I didn't know enough.
I heard your heart throbbing, as *you* waited for a new life,
But love is not around yet; I'm not surprised.
I listened to your stomach purring, but I just stood there,
Yet, I'm not ready to face your fears.
I saw your legs trembling, but *you* just remained intact,
To show to me and the others that even poverty cannot pull *you* down.
I saw your knees bending, but *you* stood there;
Helping the others that poverty kneeled.
I saw your feet freezing, but *you* kept walking;
Nothing can stop *you*.
Now; *you* heard my thoughts, for a new world,
And you're trying to fix it no matter what.
You saw me crying, for losing just a game,
But *you* held me in your hands and gave me your precious love.
You read my lips that children are dying,
But *you* remained strong and kept *me* alive.
You saw my throat swallowing the whole bread,
But *you* stood starving and said you're ok.
You heard my heart throbbing as I saw a nightmare;
But *you* remained calm and gave me a hug.
You listened to my stomach purring; as I haven't eaten all day,
But *you* gave me your food and a place to stay.
You saw my legs trembling from fear,
But *you* stood by me, over here.
You saw my knees touching the ground,
And *you* ran towards me, not letting me down.
You saw my feet freezing as I slept out tonight,
And *you* took them, warming them for me.
You and I are not equal in this world,
But your feelings can *really* touch my soul.
And *why*, this world cannot be fair?
No justice, *no* love around there.

No peace in sight today,
I'm sorry we have to wait for a brighter day.
Goodbye; I leave my last breath in front of *you,*
Please try to make the world better, at least for *you!*

Evdoxia Mavronicola (15)

BOUND BY HER

She completes me and the idea leaves my heart somewhat disturbed;
Yet not one thought of her ever escapes me.
Her love is everlasting and what a fool it turned me out to be.
To have ever loved like that, without any inseparability, no harmony.
For I put in all the effort and all it took were those three words
I was the only one listening and my voice was left shy and unheard.
Visions and fantasies of what could have been imprisoned my every thought;
The world meant nothing unless I solemnly possessed the key to her heart.
This false reality left me and the truth fiercely awoke, ripping me apart.
Our eyes meet in equal discretion and I knew I wanted to restart
Alas my heart is young and would lead me longing into pain, distraught.
I tried so hard to battle this feeling and with perseverance, I fought
But my heart was restricted by the force of a thousand chains.
The feelings she has infected my very soul with, will never leave
And alas her love has left me
With the crushing reality of a satisfaction I will never retrieve.
For her heart belongs to another now, that much was hard to believe.
I lay behind the curtains of social acceptance, confused and in pain.
And the love I had for her is hidden
And peaking over the blankets of fake emotion,
Waiting for those words to leave her mouth and enter my ear again.

Giacomo Jack Brian Ricciardi (15)

THE WORLD OF BOOKS

Books are our friends,
And constant guides.
They help us forget,
Our sorrows and chides.
They take us deep,
Into a world of joys.
In oceans of fantasies,
And lands of ploys.
Flying with fairies,
Swimming with mermaids.
Frolicking with dragons,
Keeps one busy throughout the day.
Who cares, who bothers,
If some feel real others say fiction.
For in this world,
Can there be a better action?

Ananya Jain (9)

THE REASON I WAS LATE FOR SCHOOL

My walk to school is like World War Two in only a second,
Bombs go off, policeman chase me and a whole lot more.

My walk to school is *Around the World in 80 Days* in only a minute,
The ocean roars, the trees sing and that's just a beginning.

My walk to school is like the amusement park in fifteen minutes,
A firework show, an ice cream stand and that's just to start.

My walk to school is the best thing in the world,
And that's why, each day, I only do it in thirty minutes.

But each day at school my teacher says,
'Wilona, I will not hear another excuse from you.'

Elseline Smith (13)

THIRD TIME 'ROUND

So I'm coming back for my third time 'round
Yet another chance for me to take home the crown
Another attempt to stop the eager smile
Of my anticipation collapsing down into a frown

Because I came here first with something personal
Mildly bright, designed to be thankful
It didn't work out well but I wasn't surprised
I mean I must've read 'Drinking Games' a few dozen times

And then last year I couldn't attend
So I sent along my mum to read my poem instead
It was still quite personal but now a lot darker
Far less hope and I hoped I'd get farther

But yet again I fell in the final race
Made it down to the track but couldn't keep up the pace
So yet again I find myself here between second and fiftieth bloody place
And I'm wallowing in a little bit of personal disgrace

'But big words win prizes' is what I'm telling myself
While the critic in me thinks I could've written better myself
And that's probably a lie but in a way I guess it helps
To preserve some sense of my sense of self

So this year I thought I'd be a little bit rough
Try a little bit aggressive, or a little bit tough
Something a bit different or just try hard enough
To maybe pick up the prize on my third time up

So it looks like I'm back for the third time 'round
I came here to win, I came for the crown
But I don't think I'll win so I'll settle for now
Just for the roaring applause of the crowd.

Charlie Gillen (16)

THE BOAT PEOPLE

We are where
The glassy water
Cries with the wind.
Where laughter is unheard,
Silence is welcomed.
Where we learn
The value of minutes.
We are where
All bad things
Are sequestered to.

We are where
The stoic weep,
The strong break.
Where the unknown
Is a chance for good.
Where we learn
The value of acceptance.
We are where
The cries of children
Pull us from our sanity.

We are where
The endless sky
Is our only safety.
Where beyond the waters
Lies our enemy.
Where we learn
The value of necessities.
We are where
Warmth
Is too expensive.

We are where
Babies yearn
For love and bliss.
Where loss of hope
Means suicide.
Where we learn
The value of others.
We are where
Individual survival
Is useless.

We are where
Dark waters
Churn in suffering.
Where silence respects
The ones we lost.
Where we learn
The value of desires.
We are where
The life among us
Is withering.

We are where
Fists are clenched,
And hardships endured.
Where mechanical thoughts
Are all we have.
Where we learn
The value of strength.
We are where
Each dawn
Is more then life.

We shroud in crepuscular eternity
Locked by our heritage.
Locked by our actions.
Where pain is comfort.
Where hope is discriminating.
We are where
The boat takes us.

Kirsty Rowlinson (15)

BIRCH TREE

Bark peels off the lonely birch,
Love letters to earth.
A little creek flows past, witnessing all.
The sun laughs mockingly at the creek,
As sunlight dances off the ripples.
Days pass, years pass, centuries pass,
And still the birch stands tall.
One day the sound of a motor engine
Disrupts the forest's calm silence.
Then, *crash.*
A tree falls in the calm, peaceful wood.
The humans are coming,
Disrupting earth, destroying nature.
Now the creek is dirty and sullen.
No occasional fish darts around the murky water.
Another century passes.
The wood is gone.
In its place stands a small apartment building and a little park.
Now you can sometimes hear a bird tweet.
This is not an end,
It is a new beginning.

Elodie Liebeskind-Blaufarb (9)

JUST LISTEN

You tell us
Don't kill
Money isn't everything
Care for the land that feeds you
Help the needy
Love thy neighbour
Why do you not practice what you preach?

I'm sorry it took so long to speak
Here I stand so hurt
We can't go on pretending
Not hearing the pleading cries
Broken children hurt
Seeing the scars of suffering untold

Why didn't you do something?
Really, why?

A decent life for one and all
Fairness and equality
Is what we stand for

We are not satisfied
We will not turn away
We hear the muted cries
We see the unspoken message

Treated like dogs
But still
We will take the blame
For the hate, the grief and the pain
You might think we are insane

But really
We will do that
Just for a change

Tjanana Molefe (15)

MY TEACHER - MY SOUL

Teacher is like a key,
To the locked door of knowledge and wisdom.
Where she unlocks the door and guides us throughout the room.
Finally forgotten the key?
You are ruined!

Or she is like a ventilator of a room,
Who removes bad thoughts from our minds,
And adds good thought into it.
Finally forgotten the good thoughts?
You are ruined!

Or she is like traffic signals to the drivers,
This saves us from many accidents.
Finally forgotten the traffic rules?
You are ruined!

Or she is like water to a bud,
Who turns the buds into beautiful flowers.
Finally forgotten who turned the buds into beautiful flowers?
You are ruined!

Amal Abdul Azeez (12)

SPRINGTIME!

Hooray! Welcome in the beautiful spring!
When everyone awakens from the dead,
And they spring out from the warmth of their bed.
They're greeted by many people smiling,
Near the clear, blue freshwater spring.
Forthwith lots of children are gladly led,
To green fields and parks – or so it is said.
Animals play, and insects are dancing;
The song of spring is everywhere around.
As all the brightly coloured flowers bloom,
They rest in peace by the sound of a dove.
Cats purr contentedly, few dogs do bound,
Not anywhere is there a louder boom –
For the calm of spring, is pure, true love.

Hannah Cawthorn

I WOULD . . .

I would like to paint the sound of a mouse nibbling cheese.
To listen to the wailing of a calf.
The laughter of a child.
I would like to take home a unicorn in a cigarette box.
I would like to touch the soft fur and feathers of a griffin.
I would like to paint the heat of the sun
To feel a dragon's scaly skin.
I would like to understand the way a lion prowls in the jungle.
The mystery of magic.
The coldness in an enemy's heart.
The happiness of a child getting its first pet.
The curiosity of an adventure.
The disobedience of the truth.
To paint the movement of a minotaur.

Caitlyn Begg

TEARS FOR MY DOG

I come home from school
But you're not there to greet me
I come home from soccer
But you're not there to greet me
I come home from lots of places
But you're never there to greet me
Like you used to be
Because you are gone
My best friend's gone
It's not the same
You're not replaceable
Not like other pets
A patient bark
Sometimes you gave
But now that bark is gone
But life shall go on
Even though you're gone
It just won't be the same.

Cierra Francis (8)

MY MOTHER

My mother is an angel from the sky,
Her love for me is so high.
She is full of compassion and care,
She teaches me manners and how to share.

In the darkness she is a light,
She removes all my fear and fright.
She gives endless support to me,
She works very hard for me, does she.

For every problem she finds a solution,
And with her composure, removes my confusion.
A role model for every child,
An ideal personality, so gentle and mild.

Of the wide world, I am so ignorant,
She then leads me to enlightenment.
She spreads her shade for me like a tree,
Into my future she helps me see.

She loves me a lot-
She's a blessing that I've got,
And we both love each other,
Me and my mother.

Anagha Subhash Nair (11)

SMILE

Hey, hey, you can't bring me down
I have a big smile that won't turn into a frown
because I'm as high as the sky
and you can't make me cry.

I got taught to be myself
and that is what I'm going to do
so I have to stay strong
and live my life without caring what people think of me.

You say things about me
but you just have to see
I will try not to cry
when you lie.

When you're not here
I want to cry
because I feel so lonely
and you make everything okay.

So I know for a fact
that when you smile, I smile
because it gives me hope
so no one can bring me down.

Ellie Louise Brooke

MY DRACONIC COMPANION

In the past I've tried my foul luck
With cute cats and daring dogs.
But I've decided there's no better option
Than a dragon who lights your logs.

They're noble to the end
And they play a joke or two.
The only problem being which:
They're stubborn through and through.

Despite the mentioned latter fact,
I adore my new-found friend.
His scales, his eyes, his sharpish fangs.
Our bond shall never end.

The only hard part I can think of
Is how to find these so-called dragons.
This one was found by luck alone,
Usually talked of over flagons.

I adore the way he cocks his head
With a sense of curious intent.
I cannot see how one would dread,
This harmless dragon's content.

My sharp-toothed friend still follows
Through the day and through the night.
I'm glad that I have trained him well
And he's glad I made things right.

I've tried my best to parent him.
He's tried his best to please.
That's why I've become so fond of him.
It's rather hard to find displease.

Such intelligent creatures
Who can remember the slightest source.
They hold a remarkable feature:
'You understand English?' I paused.

The dragon simply nodded,
Confirming the given test.
And with that I softly prodded:
'Clever dragon, I wont protest.'

Another story I now share with you,
It happened yesterday.
I took the dragon for a walk.
A consequence I had to pay.

For promising to take him to the lake,
I'd made a miscalculation.
I realised a day too late
And now owed him compensation.

We finally arrived there
After maybe an hour or two.
Then he started singing songs,
Draconic through and through.

The vibrations rippling the water,
Causing fish to swim about.
Glistening under midday sun,
The voice of this dragon about.

It sent a streak of warmth right down
My old yet healthy spine.
I then approached my draconic friend,
Who was still singing to the sky.

I realised it was a plea in which
He desired the act of flight.
Alas his wings weren't ready yet,
He would only fall and die.

'One day you'll fly just like them,'
I pointed to a flock of birds.
'But for now you'll have to train,
And silently observe.'

It saddened me to say it
yet I couldn't tell him lies.
I love him dearly with my heart
and one day I know he'll rise.

Dante Silver (17)

CAMPING TRIP GONE WRONG

Three young boys, Joe, John and Jake,
Once went camping down by the lake,
But there was a story they didn't believe,
About a beast that climbed tree to tree.

The beast was hairy, covered in mud,
It was hungry for raw meat and blood,
With a lion's mane and a snake as a tail,
And a hunting sense that would never fail.

The story itself was a hundred years old,
To the children the tale was told,
Campers brave enough to camp by the lake,
Would fall asleep, but never wake.

So that night, Joe, John and Jake,
Who had gone camping down by the lake,
Heard a bone-chilling howl, and turned and fled,
And then saw the beast, its eyes were red.

The beast gave chase, on the children,
All three of them thought the monster would kill them,
With an almighty roar and a scream of a child,
John and Jake wished they hadn't camped in the wild.

The darkness covered Joe's guts and gore,
But the beast wasn't satisfied; it wanted more,
The beast leapt and slashed, now John was gone,
But Jake was alive, so the beast carried on.

Now Jake was alone, tired and scared,
And the monster charged him, all fangs bared,
Jake was defenceless, he wanted to leave,
But he had one last trick up his sleeve.

Jake then grinned, his eyes turning red,
He grew claws and fangs, his skin now shed,
Now hairs burst out of him, all pitch-black,
As the werewolf howled and called for its pack.

All fifty odd wolves came to Jake's aid prowling,
Half of them roaring, half of them growling,
Now the beast turned its back and fled,
But the pack gave chase, they wanted it dead.

One juvenile werewolf grabbed its foot,
The beast couldn't move, as it was stuck,
Now Jake roared, "I've come to avenge."
Then ripped off its head and claimed his revenge!

Callum Rowe (12)

SMILE

A smile is an expression to cherish,
An expression to share and keep,
A smile is something that is brought to you through the angels of your sleep.

A face lights up with a twinkle,
You can't but help smiling back,
Scarce are the qualities we need:
a smile is what we lack.

One day when the world is an Eden,
Even though they still don't smile now,
When you are all made of happiness they will ne'er return it with frowns.

It's only so much I could tell you,
Out of a world full of envy and greed,
And I hope someday you'll realise a smile is what we so dearly need.

Through all the disasters and famines,
When all we can do is just mope,
We will soon all find out that the smile is the best sort of hope.

Zoe Smith

UNTITLED

I'm like Icarus falling to his death,
My feathers scattered in the aftermath,
Awaiting the day I take my last breath,
Inevitably chosen by my path.
My first taste of freedom leaves me condemned
Yet I know I won't change for any man
My actions, to stop myself being hemmed,
No matter what I would have always ran.
I refuse to be a marionette,
Society's puppet who cannot scream,
Being made into an army cadet.
That's why no one can tell me not to dream
And why I'd rather be myself and free,
Than have society try to change me.

Jessica Taylor

MY MAGNUM OPUS

Emptiness creates a place
For emotions to reside
Passion pours through paint
Before being condemned by unfamiliar eyes
An emulsion of colours lark to fulfil my vision
They fight with each other
Striving for recognition
Awaiting a grand commotion
Beseeching appraisal
Such is this narcissistic creation
Yet, once the prominence dies
It lingers, desolate halls
Pinned to misfortune like Christ
For you see my dear friend,
The history of my magnum opus
Is now complete.

Almeera Mujahid

NOTORIETY, UNCOVERED

A queen has her reign, and then she dies. It's inevitable.

I used to cry
at the state I had let myself come to,
but now my killings fill me with strength.
To be in power,
to have that . . . *determination*
that only the queens know,
is what I dreamt of from the prison walls.

Murder is necessary.

When we got bored
we drank all the money,
and ate the souls.
Young ones skipped around me,
standing behind,
waiting to catch the dress.
But I don't give hope,
I don't possess warmth.
Love is a line that you sing in a song,
a passing facade,
a moment of true glory and reckless affection.

We don't have room for love.

But suppose they're right?
Telling us there are those *beings* down there.
I won't talk to them,
I won't look at them.
I will do nothing but report back to me.

Ants will stay in their place.

Someone once told me,
at a party,
that knives will do the trick; the knives hidden
up the skirt
of Lady Injustice.
And if you're lucky,
very lucky,
and mostly I'm lucky,
then a slight glimmer of superiority will stab the hearts
of the ones who deserve it,
and the battle cries will fill us with re-assurance.

I don't believe in such luck.

Ethan Hemmati

213

I AM A POET

I am a poet,
I engrave my mind,
On to page after page,
Through sorrow,
Through rage,
I'm setting free words,
That were trapped in a cage
I am a poet,
I write as I think,
Write it down before I blink,
I'm running out of ink,
Ideas on the brink,
Through rhyme,
Through time,
Through the rhythm,
I'm given,
I scrap the plot,
I scrap the plan,
Does it make sense?
I don't give a damn!
I am a poet,
Scrawling now,
My hair is brown,
My eyes are blue,
Yours are too!
Like the sea we see on the shore,
Where is she?
That sells the shells,
Where you can hear the sea if you listen well,
Sand in my toes,
My ideas grow,
My imagination overflows,
I am a poet,
Do I make sense?
Even through my different tense?
Jump over the fence,
This feeling is immense,
Is the grass greener on the other side?
Or do we cut it way too fine?
Do we all drown in our own pride?
And do we dare jump out of line?
What really makes us so kind?
Is it our soul?

Our love?
Our mind?
So many questions,
It's really sublime!
I am a poet.

Tabitha Lay

METAPHORICAL WAR POEM

I crouched as if I was abducted into a parallel planet
There my related brother stood, without a piece of mind,
His shattered bones, refreshing the heart
All in a century turned kind
His jungle – like, spherical and abandoned eyes
Stared deep into my throat,
Like waves luring throughout the distant earth
Fighting to reclaim his leadership on the boat

As time dived by
He became the devil of my twin,
Hell's pit jumped into battle
As if hell was his sin
3 words avenged his forfeited mouth
Splurged onto my despicable mind,
War has had its day
And dilutes into mankind

His solid fists crunched into oblivion
And created a savaged black hole,
He glided into respect with dignity and hope
When at last I saw his soul.

Kamran Rzazada

THE FOOTBALL GAME

At the football game
           3pm in Hounslow
Bright blue kit
           With the enemies stood beside
A referee anxiously waiting
           For the important game to commence
And out on the pitch
           Roaring reds
And blooming blues.

The reds
           Left, right and centre
                  Ready for kick off
Shiny kits and boots polished to perfection
           While the blues grubby, gory
looking fearful win or lose

Everything's kicked off
           Reds to reds
                  Blues to blues
Ball in goal everyone stares
           Reds one blues nil.

Half time, shaky hands
           What are the coaches going to say
Reds are joyful, blues are scared
           Here come the coaches
Reds look up, blues look down
           Coaches shout and cheer.

Half times ended
           The crowd cheer them on
The pitch is still
           as penalty time takes place
Blues score, here's a draw.

For that second
           The war was settled
In an instant
           Both teams huddled together
Anyone would think
           friends not enemies.

Melissa Hyde

216

BETRAYAL OF A SAILOR

He was a lonely sailor
Living a saddened life
Happiness is what he wished for
Another maiden, for wife

The love of his life was gone
Another he desired
He prayed early each dawn
Until she was acquired

He came across a lady
Upon the sandy gold beach
She was his eye candy
Love was in reach

Her eyes were so beautiful
Her hair so lovely
She looked so very wonderful
But wasn't what she seemed

They set sail upon his ship
Out far into the sea
He said, I'll never leave you'
Said she, I'll curse thee'

For she stole his loving heart
Then showed her colours true
For she was oh so smart, so smart
Drowned him in the blue

Scott Somerville

I LOVE HIM

I miss him, but he does not know it,
I'd fight for him but I cannot show it,
My love for him is as strong as ever,
It shall never fade; not now, not ever.
I love him but; I do not want to,
I genuinely don't know what to do,
Hope is all that's left for me,
I love you! Don't you see?

Beth Purvis

THE LAMENT

A scientist might see rods and cones,
A pathway to the brain,
An artist might see two black mirrors,
Reflecting wind and rain,
A philosopher he would see the answers,
Locked away in the head up there,
Yet I see glorious, resplendent beauty,
Perfect, serene and fair.

A stylist would see the ultimate tool,
Luscious, light and pure,
A photographer he would see pure gold,
Waiting to be procured,
Yet I see a different kind of gold,
Priceless, soft and unique,
I see the vibrant quality of her character,
Matched only by physique.

A perfectionist, in his state of mind,
Would have trouble finding fault,
A pessimist, in the darkest of days,
Couldn't help but think happy thoughts,
I sometimes wonder why I would
Give it all up for a girl,
Then I take one look, and just stand and think,
I'd follow her into Hell.

Jack Duffield

THE TRANSITIONS OF LIFE

I was once a child to, y'know,
Oh how I miss those good old days,
When it was play play play, and laugh all day,
Why couldn't my childhood stay?

I had a childhood too, y'know,
Back when life was fun,
But now it's all done like the sad setting sun,
It's a battle that could not be won,

It wasn't an easy thing, y'know,
Growing up I mean of course,
With GCSEs and no room to breathe,
Makes it all hard to achieve,

My time is almost gone, y'know,
My last poem before I'm done,
Coz with this last bit of fun and a new setting sun,
It's time to find my loved one,

I'll have no time to grieve, y'know,
Coz surely I'll have a son,
I'll watch him have fun under his setting sun,
For the cycle must go on.

Richard J C Smith

MY ONE TRUE ROSE

A rose is a thing of beauty,
A beacon for delicacy,
Red, for blood, lust, love,
As symbolic as the dove,

But the rose I'm thinking of,
Is the blush of your cheeks,
Your lips as they shine,
Your heart as it beats,
Making you mine,

Yet, the thorns are still there,
The bumps in the road,
The pain in my side,
The hate as we know,
Our jealousy and pride,

My rose is the hope we hold on to,
As each petal falls a new chapter begins,
With the thorns in our side as we struggle,
But we never let the good moments go,
The essence of us creates a new rose,
To begin a new life of balance as we know,
Our rose remains whole,
As our journey continues and as we grow.

Jasmine Womack

A NIGHT IN THE LIGHT

It was a ballistic night in the city of New York
And there I was in the diner fiddling with my fork.
As I left the diner the loveliest ladies were walking by,
In their gorgeous dresses and their *immensely* high heels.
Walking down the streets of the city that never sleeps,
Was like, golden, blessed heaven on earth.
The bright, glitzing lights glowed with pride very evenly.
My two beautiful, fantastic eyes had never seen such an
Inspiring place. In my head I thought, New York City
Is a dream which can't be replaced by any other place
Made by us, determined, wise humans.

Adriana Hasa

220

THE WINTER SCENE

The flakes perched on the winter wonderland carpet.
A throng of whiteness covering the ferny floor.
The phantom listeners sprinkling their woes.
The fresh-baked cake covered in sugary icing.
The thrill of excitement rushes down my spine.
The yeti in the snow is the camel of the desert.
The trees bow down in grace, praising their new decorations.
Nature awakes to the serenity of the world.
Covered in a thick, white, fluffy blanket.
A passer-by trudges through the fresh laid-snow,
Marking their track wherever they go.
Playful children giggle with glee
As their snowballs meet their target!
I take one last glimpse over my shoulder,
As I appreciate the phenomenal wintry scenes.

Har-Charan Kaur Takhar

CHANGE

The thought of change; it terrifies.
No limit to its power

In the turns of time,
In the loops of childhood,
In the plummet of fear and uncertainty

It races along with time, both wild, determined
Incapable of being restrained

Erratic, like the lone, wild creature
But it need not be alone
It simply needs embraced

Drop your net,
don't try restrain what can't
Dance in the aftermath,
Breathe in the same old oxygen with new eyes.

Lauren Palmer

MUSIC

The words unravel like expensive silk,
Rolling through my ear drums,
Instructions for me to move my feet,
I read between the lyrics,
Hearing the artists emotions,
Take over my body,
The words, the tune, the funky beat,
A gushing waterfall of everything I love,
In an amazing song.

Instead of the yucky red stuff my veins fill with music,
It's like the artist speaks to me,
Turning into my brain,
Controlling me,
And every part inside me,
Just wants to let go,
Scream at the top of my voice,
Chanting the words repeatedly,
Dance until it hurts,
Collapse on the floor and cry,
Sharing every moment with the beautiful writer.

It reads my mind and solves my problems,
Listening like a mother,
Caring like a father,
Sharing like a sister,
Speaking like a brother,
I talk to it by staying silent,
Letting it move me slowly.

There are lots of different songs,
Slow, quick, happy, sad, exciting, eye-opening,
But each one like a person,
Is unique and beautiful,
It,
Like a book,
Tells a story,
A one like life never ending and complicated.

Music is brave and selfless,
Only existing for the happiness of others,
Not caring for itself,
It relaxes me and agrees with me and when I'm wrong,
It's forgiving,
Helpful.

Music is a good friend,
There when I need it,
When I want it,
It puts a smile on my face,
Songs teach me lessons,
Each song shares the same message,
That everything will turn out ok,
That I will be safe.

It makes me happy,
It makes me sad,
It reminds me,
It won't judge me or hurt me,
It is my new friend,
Music, music, music, music . . .

Casey Jane Sickling

SOLACE

I smell my salty tears fall on my face again,
I smell the stench of alcohol drifting down the corridor,
I smell his sick covered feet behind the door,
I smell his harsh smell flaring my nostrils,
I hear him stumble into the room and pushing past the furniture in a fury,
I hear a picture frame smash on the floor and trampled on,
I hear his taunting laugh echoing across the room,
I hear his nearing footsteps drumming into my ear . . .
I see his snarled face look at me with a devilish glare,
I see him shouting at me but there is deafness now to my ears,
I see him reach for his warning bat in the corner,
I see him grab me and slap my face as I try to escape,
I taste my blood in my mouth as I cry for mercy,
I taste the bitter words that spit on me with every breath,
I taste the dust on the floor as my body is crushed,
I taste the screams escaping my mouth but hearing only a whisper,
I feel the heavy blows on my head,
I feel his tears singe my skin as he batters me,
I feel my last breath escape my body;
I feel nothing.

Jassimran Doklu

STRONG?

Don't judge the girl that you see,
Because that's not the real me,

You don't have a clue,
About what's fake and what's true,
You don't see past the make-up and fake smiles, don't see the tears in her eyes,
If you looked further, maybe you'd realise,
That she's the girl, who cries herself to sleep at night,
Just because once again something didn't go right,
She's the girl who pretends to be strong,
Who is so used to everything going wrong,
Is used to never being good enough,
Used to always looking rough,
Because she hasn't slept,
Because she stayed up the whole night and wept,
She puts in her headphones, turns the music up loud,
Wishing she could just be herself and be proud,
Instead she wishes she could be the girl they all want her to be,
She asks herself 'what's wrong with being me?'
She'll wonder who would miss her, if she wasn't around any longer,
She'll wish that she wasn't so down, she'll wish that she was stronger,
If only someone could see what's going on,
Everyone believes her lies, that's she's being strong,
No-one would believe it; they wouldn't believe she was depressed,
People throw that word around, when really they're only stressed,

Depressed is the emptiness that never goes away,
Waking up in the morning, only to dread the coming day,
The feeling of aloneness, knowing no-one could ever understand,
The need for someone to just hold your hand,
The want to just be held while you cry,
For someone to listen, while you let it all spill out, talk until the words run dry,
So you see, she's not the girl you think she is, the girl you think you know,
If only you knew what she'd do to be her, or how far she'd go,
Just to not live life so unhappy, and so messed up inside,
If only you knew, how many tears she's cried,
How many times she's held the knife to her wrist,
And tried to make herself believe she'd be missed,
How many times she said 'I'm done' yet carried on trying,
Because deep down she knows, it has to be better than this slowly dying,
If you looked into her eyes, you'd see they hide a world of pain,
If you think she's happy then think again,

A smile can say a thousand things, but only if it's real,
It can't say those thousand things, if they're not what you truly feel,
She'll bring her legs to her chest, curl up in a ball, and let it out,
She can't hold it any longer, she's going to cry, scream and shout,
You might not want to listen, but she's going to make sure you hear,
Once someone else understands, she'll have nothing to fear,
So please don't turn your back on her, please stay and help her realise,
That she's not the only one to feel this way, and it's not a big surprise,
For someone so young to be so messed up in these ways,
Because teenage depression is so common these days.

Vickie O'Sullivan

THE LONE SOLDIER

'Cause I am a lone soldier,
     I'll stand on my own two feet.
          For the ones that I love,
               I'll lift up my hand with the gun.

Each shot I wilfully fire,
     echoes throughout my cold world.
          Emotions? I have none;
               it is this, my duty to do.

No tears shall form in my eyes,
     there's none left for me to weep,
          they died out in the past
               my friends and allies alike.

No dead body will move me,
     for now my heart is pure steel.
          All emotions will rust;
               this is the cruel world which I live.

I move onto the next zone,
     Never turning to look back.
          Knowing that I stand alone;
               for I am the lone soldier.

Isabel Latimer

THE RAIN STICK

Upend the rain stick and what happens next? Water trickling
Out from a dripping tap, a soft diminuendo, as light
As a dewdrop, yet suddenly, a sizzling, like sausages

On a barbecue, fizzing and pushing past, competing to get to
The end of the stick. Next a crescendo, like an army
Of angry ants in hobnail boots stamping about on

Rocks, booming, a sudden downpour, a raging storm,
Then . . . silence. Upend the stick again. Tropical
Rainforest air comes rushing out of this strange bumpy

Tube, a stubbly chin belonging to a man who has lost his
Razor, this heavy stick, an ugly cactus plant with pushed-in spines,
Filled with ugly black grit, but the sound!
                              Remarkable!

Zahra Abbasi (10)

FORWARD POETRY INFORMATION

We hope you have enjoyed reading this book - and that you will continue to enjoy it in the coming years.

If you like reading and writing poetry drop us a line, or give us a call, and we'll send you a free information pack.

Alternatively if you would like to order further copies of this book or any of our other titles, then please give us a call or log onto our website at www.forwardpoetry.co.uk.

Forward Poetry Information
Remus House
Coltsfoot Drive
Peterborough
PE2 9BF
(01733) 890099